VIRTUOSOS
OF
JUGGLING

FROM THE MING DYNASTY
TO CIRQUE DU SOLEIL

Karl-Heinz Ziethen
Alessandro Serena

Published by

RENEGADE
JUGGLING
www.renegadejuggling.com

Renegade Juggling
PO Box 406
Santa Cruz, CA 95061
USA
www.renegadejuggling.com

WRITTEN BY: Karl-Heinz Ziethen, Alessandro Serena
   Luci della Giocoleria published 2002 by Stampa Alternativa/Nuovi Equilibri, Italy
FOREIGN EDITOR: Adolfo Rossomando
TRANSLATED BY: Anthony Trahair
EDITOR: Robert Ward
DESIGN & TYPOGRAPHY: Diane Rigoli, www.rigoliartstudio.com

ISBN: 0-9741848-0-2

10 9 8 7 6 5 4 3 2 1

FIRST PRINTING

Printed in China through Palace Press International

FRONT COVER: Francis Brunn, Puerto Rico, 1979
BACK COVER (clockwise from upper left): Ernest Montego, Anthony Gatto,
   Mike Chirrick, Enrico Rastelli.

CONTENTS

PREFACE

Even if one's heart and eyes have experienced a little too much over the years, the artistic display of the juggler always manages to surprise anew. Where does the secret of this most enchanting of arts lie? Is it in the variety of the production, the colorful, sparkling glitter of the presentation, the continuous surprise of successive tricks, or has it deeper roots? One would like to think so.

Something from youth remains in every adult, and the instinct for flirtation with possibility persists. Even if these feelings lie very deep down, a little encouragement can be enough to bring them to the surface.

Juggling has the appearance of a youthful enterprise, an activity evolved from skills first learned by children at play. Tossing balls, spinning hoops, or playing with a diabolo— all these games point in the direction of childhood and youth, yet it can take a lifetime to further develop these abilities into the skills attained by a true juggler. Because youth is a universal experience, it comes as no surprise that only a minority of jugglers have inherited their artistic blood. True, some have come from circus families, but even the children of circus artists usually learn all sorts of performing arts, not just juggling.

"Please kindly let me know how much you charge for one lesson in juggling so that I can have a juggler at next Saturday's club meeting." This was a letter that the famous Kara received one day, proving how naive many people are about the level of skill needed to master the juggling art. Juggling is one of the most laborious professions and, because of its dependence on split-second timing, is perhaps the most difficult of all the performing arts.

Over the centuries there have been many juggling artists who have entertained and brightened up people's lives with their original acts. Only a few, however, have managed to arouse the highest degree of amazement. Still, juggling, from its earliest beginnings, has offered unlimited possibilities and variations.

Only the most skillful juggler can fully explore the abundant potential diversity in this art. Few spectators can imagine the perseverance and strength of nerve that it requires to be an artist of this kind. It is not uncommon for a master juggler to practice a single trick

THE AUTHORS ALESSANDRO SERENA & KARL-HEINZ ZIETHEN

for more than a year before he or she feels confident enough to perform it in public. A stage performance that lasts ten minutes may have taken a lifetime of continuous, ambitious work to perfect. The spectator enjoying the show cannot comprehend the sacrifice that this sort of artistic performance demands, nor does the artist expect the audience to understand.

Superior juggling performances contain elements of beauty and elegance that originate only in the creativity of the performer. The creator has, through untiring effort, love, and total devotion, achieved perfection. An artist builds the performance from his or her own strength, initiative, and courage, and the largest sum of money cannot buy the ability to perform even the simplest juggling trick.

Unlike many acrobats, who try to emphasize the difficulty of their feats, the juggler aims to do the exact opposite—to present the difficult act as if it were the easiest thing in the world to do. The easier and more elegant the balancing or juggling appears to be, the greater the proficiency of the juggler. Juggling does not negate, or defy, the laws of gravity. Rather, the total opposite is true: juggling confirms physical and mathematical laws and formulas. But the juggler has no scientific knowledge of these; rather, the juggler creates his or her act instinctively. Like a painter or an architect who uses pictorial thinking, the juggler develops tricks from intuition and an inborn sense of balance.

Juggling is the most aesthetically enchanting form of play. In this work, I investigate what artists have achieved in juggling over the last four thousand years. A great deal of testimony to jugglers' inventiveness, hard work, and ambition is to be found in this book.

This long-awaited book is an expansion of my two-volume encyclopedia *4,000 Years of Juggling*, published in 1981. I am deeply grateful that Alessandro Serena, from Italy, worked on this latest book together with me. His knowledge about circus, theatre, and the artists' historiography is enormous.

Finally, I would like to thank Tom Kidwell (Renegade Juggling) for publishing this book, which is in fact a larger, more expansive edition of a smaller book originally published by Stampa Alternativa/Nuovi Equilibri in Viterbo, Italy, in 2002 and entitled *Luci della Giocoleria*.

—Karl-Heinz Ziethen

✤   ✤   ✤   ✤   ✤

Coming from a circus family, a few years ago while I was preparing for a look into the exam of theatrical iconography at the DAMS (art and music school), I asked Professor Picchi if I could deal with a circus argument. He had recently been amazed by an illustration from the early 1800's, which showed a group of people in a restaurant (The Perezoff) who threw plates, glasses and other household items at each other which gave him the idea of juggling. I then decided to focus on the outstanding Italian juggler Enrico Rastelli. In this way I started my research on the great Italian artist. Following this, impassioned by the subject, I proposed to my professor—Claudio Meldolesi—that I start a more detailed research for my degree thesis, extending to the performances for the mass, the folk-performances, a part of history rather neglected—particularly regarding those which are called "ring disciplines." He accepted this and I started an even more demanding study. The works of this theme are almost all foreign (not Italian) and very hard to get hold of; in Italy there aren't any places with records. Luckily having been born and grown up in a circus, I was always surrounded by artists of all sorts. Furthermore, my job (casting for all types of events), allowed me to travel extensively and to meet a great deal of professionals, among whom were some of the most important jugglers. I was thus able to collect a noteworthy heap of documentation, photographs, books and magazine articles. Furthermore I found hall programmes, registries, even had a coffee and a chat with the persons and their ancestors directly. Above all I was able to get to know Karl-Heinz Ziethen, the juggling "guru", with whom I prepared this book. The thesis was greatly liked by the university commission, which allowed me to finish university with the highest grades. From then on I have continued to collect information and I've displayed the results of my research in a certain number of books and magazines. For this, some of the considerations that you can read here have already appeared in some form or other elsewhere. However, the attention and popularity that juggling has acknowledged in the last years, and with the press coverage that it is getting, this has made it necessary to write a publication that sketches out the development of the discipline—illustrating the ability to wonder and entertain. The work thus starts with a brief analysis of the first finding of the juggling goings-on. We then pass on to Ancient Rome, to Byzantine and then to China. Returning to Europe and to the Medieval Fairs. We wait a while with the permanent circuses and the horseback variety shows, between the eighth and ninth centuries, perhaps the golden age for jugglers. In those years we recount the great figures, dedicating a long chapter on the Italian Enrico Rastelli and his followers. There are details of how juggling may have been inspired by military uniforms, restaurants, comedy, sport and leisure activities. How it may also have inspired the first silent and black and white films. We then analyse the post-war period and the great schools of Russia and China, up until the present day. We then mention the explosion of street juggling, to the rebirth of the traditional circus and the use of juggling in other contexts. Finally we describe the definitions of the new markets, the new ways of staging and we recount the new "revolutionaries" in the disciplines. Many of the feats described are taken from antique drawings and old photographs. Remember that often the images of these performances were exaggerated—we have placed a particular attention in choosing the feats documented by more than one finding. To make the comprehension easier, all the acts are described in the simplest way possible, avoiding the use of technical terms, even if they exist. It doesn't deal with juggling techniques but is an anthology of profiles of the virtuous in physical arts. A legion of modest and great artists, athletes, heroes (who were frequently anonymous), who, in recognition of their creativity, have met the goodwill of the public of all ages throughout the world. It isn't even a taxonomical work, neither a "dictionary" of jugglers pretending to be complete. The material is so vast that we are already thinking about other publications to deepen other themes and to illustrate the innovative results of jugglers in the last two or three decades.

From 1996 I entertained myself with the editing of CIRCO, the only Italian magazine dedicated to circus, and I have dug deeply into its archives, among one of the most ample in our country. A big thanks goes out to: Edigio Palmiri, to the long list of collaborators and publishers (in various ages), Claudio Monti and Raffaele De Ritis. Beyond my family, to whom I give a big hug, I would like to express my gratitude to my friends and all the women who have put up with hours and hours of tedious (for them) research in dusty antique bookshops all over the world. Particularly David, Giorgio, Francesco, Iris, Susanna, Anna and Sabrina. Respect also goes out to Emilio and Gigi—comrades in other publishing works. Lastly I would like to thank Adolf, without whose presence this book would have never existed.

I must thank the numerous foreign correspondents that I bothered asking for help and advice. I would also like to acknowledge Markschiess van Trix and Hermann Sagemüller, assiduous German archivists, and Greg Parkinson and Fred Dahlinger, director and archive manager respectively of the Baraboo Circus World Museum, Wisconsin, for some rare documents concerning European jugglers on tour in America. Also Kirk Andrews, from the London Theatre Museum, for all the information regarding the English music halls in the 1920's.

Thanks also to Giancarlo Pretini, who has put together (and co-ordinated for the benefit of all the students of the folk-shows, present and future) an incredible amount of material, which has been very encouraging to new researchers. My research started long ago and a few gentlemen and educated men of the circus, who had encouraged me at the start, are, unfortunately, no longer with us. Among these are Antonio Arcudi, Pierre Paret, and particularly Massimo Alberini, who for half a century wrote about the circus with exemplary seriousness in the Italian newspaper *Corriere della Sera*, and with who's life's work has been an example to follow for all of us. In addition too, a huge thanks to these men and women for their valuable suggestions. In our hearts will always be their fond memories.

—Alessandro Serena

I

FROM SACRED TO PROFANE

ANCIENT TRACES

Circus only started its life in about 1770 AD, but the disciplines we see today, especially those called "circus skills," are ancient. Traces of these skills have been found in many countries, right from the start of civilization. The oldest exhibition of such seems to be that of graffiti, found in the tomb of Ben Hassani, dating back to 2040 BC. Although folk-performances are generally associated with nomadic movements, it appears that the first jugglers performed almost exclusively in fixed locations.

The Greek philosopher, Zeno, from Elea, in documentation from 422 AD describes a banquet of the rich Athenian, Kallias, who, aiming to entertain his guests had invited a group of artists from Siracusa (Sicily). Amongst the group was a woman who amazed this noble gathering by juggling 12 rings.

In 324 AD, Quinto Curzio Rufo, Alexander Magnus' historian, describes that the king, during an attempt at conquering India, witnessed and admired an Indian "country juggler." This juggler was learned in the art of tossing tiny peas that from a distance "passed through the eye of a needle."

BAKED CLAY, THEBEN 200 B.C.

Additionally, a very ancient terra-cotta statue from Tebe, dating around 200 AD, represents an artist engaged in the act of juggling and the equilibrium curiously similar to that which Enrico Rastelli might have performed 1800 years later. From then on, pictures of plates, paintings, frescos, relieves, bronze and stone sculptures have borne witness to the presence of jugglers in the various historic periods and the influence that they had on the people, the craftsmen, and the artists.

In many inscriptions, numerous references have been found to jugglers or so it has been presumed. From one of these, for example, dated around 100 AD, we learn that the Roman Tagatus "Pilicrepus" Ursus, also known as King of the Ball, was the first self-acclaimed juggler to use a glass ball.[1]

IN THE SHADOW OF THE GLADIATORS

The doctrine of Panem and Circenses made itself known in Rome with the incredible glamour of colossal performances. In between the bloody games in the ring, jugglers and acrobats were often called to entertain the crowds. It seems that the regulars of the hot baths, a more-refined public to those of the large amphitheaters, particularly enjoyed the jugglers. The ancient Romans, however, were more precise and taxonomic with a larger vocabulary.

RELIEF IN AN ATTIC TOMB

The Latin Chancellor, Marcus Fabio Quintilianus, around 90 AD, wrote how the term *ventilator* was a general way of describing "he who threw and caught objects," while the words *pilarius* and *pilicrepus* (in Latin *pila* means ball) mean "he who played with spherical objects." There are many references to these disciplines.

In the first century BC, the Latin poet, Marcus Valerians Marziale, wrote in his *Liber Spectacolorum*, on the occasion of the unveiling of the Coliseum (then called the Amphitheatre Flavius), 16 poems dedicated to all the "showbiz" disciplines. Quite clear indications of the ancient juggling activity can be found in authoritative Jewish sources at about the same time. The *Talmud* bears witness a number of times to the work of jugglers. For example, it is stated that Simeon Ben Gamaliel was able to "take eight lit torches, throw them in the air, catch one and throw that one in the air without touching the others."

It seems that this type of work was carried out in front of temples to entertain the pilgrims who came to the capital to celebrate the main festivities. This custom came to an end when the Romans invaded and destroyed Jerusalem. Meanwhile in Rome, the lazy days for the jugglers ended with the collapse of the Roman Empire and the advent of Christianity. The fathers of the church (Tertullianus leading with his De Spectaculus) associated any type of entertainment with the cruel amphitheatric games and tried their hardest to stop the spread.

Other reasons for the condemnation by Christianity to all forms of entertainment derived from the "idolization" of the actors and the presumed uselessness of the shows. In this way, in those years of hard persecution, there began an exodus of artists that ended up becoming a nomadic populace.

CHRISTIANITY AND THE EXODUS TO BISANZIO

The artistic populace moved to Bisanzio, where the Royal Court continued to organize great performances and entertainment of all sorts and where jugglers were among the most appreciated. Later, the city was chosen as the stable residency of Constantine, giving it the name Constantinople and making it the last great capital of the Roman Empire. Here the recreational traditions of the Romans were almost completely inherited.

John Crisostomo Patrarca, living in the metropolis in the fourth century AD, left a description of jugglers, even if contrary. A juggler may have been Saint Sidonius Apollinare, a Gaulish-Roman priest and

EGYPTIAN WALL PAINTING, CA. 2040 B.C.

author around 480 AD.[2] While he was head of the resistance against the Visigoths, he distracted his men by juggling with four balls in order to maintain high morale. Constantinople was the first place to complete intercultural exchanges between eastern and western artists. The Asiatic peoples, particularly the Chinese, already had their juggling tradition well founded.

CONFUCIUS AND THE JUGGLER-WARRIORS

Throughout Asia, there have been finds indicating the ancient presence of jugglers through books, paintings, wooden and stone sculptures and objects from tombs. In China, for instance, the first juggling feats came about from daily life. Fights between tribes, hunting scenes or working moments became transformed into rituals whereby juggling was viewed as spectacular events.

It seems that juggling spread partly due to the use of boomerangs as a hunting and war instrument. When resting, the warriors and the hunters occupied themselves in tough competition with the double aim of keeping in training and electing the best amongst them. In time, these demonstrations of skill ended up dropping the athletic component in favor of leisure, becoming true and exciting performances.

Some warrior-artists quickly mastered juggling up to five boomerangs at the same time. They adopted thereafter other tools such as the "light tridents" or the "rotating meteors." The foremost, inspired by war scenes, were blunted battle staffs that were used much like modern flag bearers. The idea of the rotating meteors came from daily life. They were containers full of water tied together by a long rope and spun at incredible speeds without spilling a drop. Depending on the historic period, the public was made up of representatives of the upper and lower classes. In China, juggling had exceptional admirers—the Taoist Zhuang Zi tells us in a proposal of Confucius that he was amazed at observing the expertise of a juggler:

"When Confucius passed Chu, he arrived in a forest where he saw a hunchback that caught cicada with sticks that he held between his fingers. 'Your dexterity is grand,' exclaimed Confucius, 'How did you arrive at such a result?'

'It is the fruit borne of a long training,' replied the hunchback. 'I practiced for five or six months with two balls, one on top of the other on top of a long stick. If they don't fall, it means that not many cicadas will escape from me. When I'm able to keep three in equilibrium, it will mean that I'll be able to catch them even with my bare hands.' "[3]

The same Zhuang Zi tells of Xiong Yiliao, then commander of the army of the king of the Chou Dynasty, who showed the enemy soldiers, the Song, his famous nine juggling balls. Amazed by his grand ability as leader, and afraid of this, the Song surrendered without even attempting to battle.[4]

CHINESE JUGGLER, QING DYNASTY

It was the Han Dynasty (220 BC-206 AD), which assured China the period of major growth in each economic field. Attention was given to the disciplines of the folk-performances, which were unified with the nobler, under the definition of the "100 Games." The 100 Games were a series of competitions in which the most excellent participated in every category. Within the disciplines there were juggling, singing, sound mimicking, acting, dance and all else that could make up the components of the games and performances. Seems therefore that the codification of the various folk-performances happened before those in the western world.

The 100 Games were celebrated inside grand festivities for the arrival of dignitaries or foreign diplomats in which, other than the normal exchanging of gifts, sumptuous performances took place. From the analysis of a stone engraving, dating from the third century AD, which illustrated one of these performances, we can draw observations about the evolution that took place in those years of juggling. Touched upon was the "dance of the seven plates," that could be defined as the progenies of the plate routines practiced today. Also famous was juggling with five different weapons: ax, lance, sword, halberd and arc.

Jar juggling also made a big name for itself. Here the artists juggled with huge porcelain jars finely worked with a weighting around 33-44 pounds. When the large objects descended, they were caught on the back of their neck, then they put them on their forehead and, with an energetic push with

CHINESE JUGGLERS, HAN DYNASTY

their hands, made them turn around like an enormous spinning top, with the base always on their cranium.

With the fall of the Han Dynasty, hard times returned for the artists of the folk-performances, forced to perform in the streets and put up with long moves in a nation tormented by violent battles. It was the Tang Dynasty (from 618 AD) that brought the country back to a good level of culture and prosperity, while in Europe at the same time the long and dark medieval period started.

THE EAST AND WEST IN THE MEDIEVAL PERIOD

In the medieval period, the largest witness of the presence of jugglers and jesters is owed to the manuscripts of monks who, testifying their firm position against every form of spectacle, confirmed, however, the prosperous and widespread presence of jugglers and jesters. Even so, the word juggler seems to have entered its current-day meaning in the medieval era. It derives from the same root-word of jester, in French *jongleur* is a synonym and is from the Latin *joculator*, a term designating any type of ambulant artist. Therefore mountebanks and troubadours (singers and minstrels) traveled to the squares and courts to entertain the heterogeneous public of that time. Also, in a generic way, musicians, poets, mime artists, charlatans, horse riders, acrobats, and "anyone who earned his living working in front of a public."[5]

Jesters carried out their profession hunting out offerings in distant villages, in squares and in markets or even engaged by rich nobles for festive celebrations. An important treatise of the 12th century put together in a unique category; "theatrical," all spectacular

JUGGLER AND MUSICIAN, MIDDLE AGES

JUGGLER AND MUSICIAN, MIDDLE AGES

activity of the jesters.[6] Soon after, there was a segregation between he who demonstrated above all his corporeity and he who on the other hand trusted himself to poetry or to music for his survival. The "jesters of the mouth," poets of the lives of saints or of heroes in stories of adventure, won good social condition, whereas jugglers, acrobats, and mountebanks remained in the margins of the society. It was this last type, touring from castle, courts and palaces, that kept alive the already ancient traditions, passing the techniques from generation in generation.

It remains difficult to think that in those hard times there could have been developments in their disciplines and yet numerous documents witness how medieval jugglers were already similar to those of our days. An illustration from the 10th century represents an Anglo-Saxon artist who juggles with three balls and three knives, while a French book from the same period contains a drawing of a juggler at work with five balls.

Juggling continued to play with the fantasy of writers and narrators, who often used them in positive connotations for tales almost fairy like. One example tells of how the Norwegian king Olaf Frygesson may have been able to juggle with three short sharp lances, when the weapons were tools in daily life.

Furthermore, in France there was the well-known tale of "the juggler of our Lady Mary." The tale narrates how a French juggler-jester called Jean Vapeur, tired of living in the margins of society, decided to adopt a religious way of life for himself. Remembering the way that the men of the church looked upon these folk-performances, he was accepted with much reserve. One night, after ceremonies offered to the Madonna, he was found practicing his art in front of the altar. A similar gesture was judged sacrilege. Jean Vapeur admitted his errors but was justified saying that not having anything else to offer the Madonna he thought at least of giving his art. Following these declarations he was pardoned and from that day on, written on the portal of the church, one can read "Hic Jacet iocolator Marie, artifex candidus Vapor Loannes." (Here lies the juggler of our Lady Mary, the humble artist Jean Vapeur.)[7]

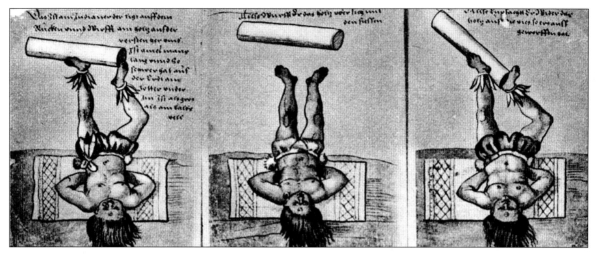

AZTEC FOOT JUGGLER, CA. 1530

The first really modern juggler, whose activity has been documented well, was the Frenchman Pierre Gringoire born in Caen (1438-1475). In some illustrations Grignoire is shown in tights, with a bag of equipment tied to his belt, while he juggled with three cubic objects in one hand. In those years, Europe started to hear about what was happening in the other continents.

Herman Cortez in 1520, returning from some of his Mexican raids, brought parchments to the court of Charles V giving information of performances, similar to the European, in those far-off countries. One parchment contained an illustration of an American Indian, lying on his back, juggling a long beam with his feet (the artists that lie on their backs juggling with their feet are called antipodists). Similar illustrations were brought to Europe a few years later, in 1528, when the German traveler Christoph Weiditz returned from the Americas with drawings that he himself had produced.[8]

On the other hand, the American Indian's activity of throwing and catching objects was also carried out by Eskimos, Algonquins, Bannock, Shoshones, Shasta, Ute and Zuni, long before the arrival of the white man.

CHINA AND THE RULE OF GENGHIS KHAN

In the meantime in China, with the coming of the Tang Dynasty (618-907), peace had returned and with it a good level of well being and culture. In the first half of the 700's the emperor Xuanzong created the celebrated "Garden of Peri," the first institute of performing arts in history, where they taught all the performance disciplines: music, song, dance and acrobatics. On one side, the young engaged in vocalization, on another side, jugglers engaged in fast but essential movements, and at yet another part, makeup artists worked on the face of an actor and so on. There was also a plan for the nationalization of juggling.

The acrobatic and juggling companies were in fact either state-owned or private. The foremost exhibited the best talents and only on the emperor's orders. The latter continued traveling around fairs and markets rejoicing, however, in the newfound interest in their art. These conditions favored a further development in juggling. In an interesting painting from that period there is, for example, an artist who juggles with six sharpened swords, with a seventh balanced on his forehead—quite an incredible feat.

Players in this renaissance of eastern juggling were also women. In a parchment from 1100 AD, there are drawings of jugglers engaged in tightrope walking. One of these is drawn in the act of juggling with 11 small balls. The imperial reporters tell us that juggling with the large jars continued to be of great success, and that the jugglers were in a continuous search for new props.[9] In this way, drumsticks, bottles, bells and even ladles were used.

In those years developed a sport similar to football that inspired the birth of a new juggling form where one could catch the balls with everything, with the exception of the feet. In the same period, Kouen-Gen invented a child's toy and later on this was to be known as the diabolo in the west, becoming a juggler's prop.

If in the west the religious had slowed the development of the physical arts, in the east, on the contrary it was normal for the Buddhist monks to use acrobatic performances to attract and entertain the crowds to spread their beliefs. The courtyards of the monasteries became delegated places for the course of the 100 Games. The spread of Buddhism was accompanied with that of juggling.

In 1215, five years after becoming the Mongol emperor, Genghis Khan conquered China and also Peking. Thereafter, there took place relevant intercultural exchanges not only inter-Asian but also between east and west.[10] Also, in this period, there are descriptions of jugglers and contortionists admired by Marco Polo personally at a feast given by Kublai Khan (emperor from 1260 to 1294).

It was during this period that the Chinese culture was absorbed in a large way by Japan, Birmania, and by the very same Mongolia, spreading, with every probability, also the multitude of traditions of the performing arts. It was, however, in 1368 that, with the start of the Ming Dynasty, juggling left the favor of the royal courts once more.

JUGGLING IN JAPAN

Many Japanese feats represented very old traditions. These include a balancing feat performed with a block of wood as well as tricks performed with a paper umbrella. In one of the latter, the juggler throws a ball into the air and catches it on top of an open umbrella, and then, by rapidly turning the handle, causes the ball to run around the umbrella's edge. Similar feats are performed with curtain rings and coins: the smaller and lighter the coin, the more difficult the feat. A Japanese silk drawing shows another traditional prop, the "kagomari" ("bottomless basket").

A 19th-century French ambassador saw at a fair in Osaka, Japan, a juggler who covered a full cup of tea with a saucer and balanced it on a long pole placed on his forehead. Gently he set the pole spinning, so that the tea started to trickle out. Another juggler balanced a three-pointed stick with three linen bags hanging down from it, then juggled small balls which repeatedly found their way into the bags. The ambassador was particularly impressed by a street performer in Fukagawa. After gathering an audience with a wild dance in a lion costume, he

JAPANESE JUGGLER WITH A BOTTOMLESS BASKET, 1876

tore off the costume and showed his juggling tricks. He took a drumstick and balanced it on one finger. On top of that he then placed a second stick, and then laid a third across the top, before going into a juggle with all three, spinning them very fast. Unexpectedly, he produced three balls and proceeded to juggle all six objects at the same time.

Japanese juggling props all have a specific meaning. The sticks are in fact drumsticks, and the juggler often incorporates drumming and singing into his performance. A ring symbolizes wealth, a balance stands for "a strong house," a spinning parasol means "thinking of finding solutions." Jugglers would be invited to such occasions as weddings, births and housewarming parties, in order to perform their tricks, which were supposed to bring luck. That indeed was what they were paid for—the enjoyment of the spectators was of secondary importance, which explains why a Japanese audience is likely to observe in silence, showing no reaction and not applauding.

FAIRS, COMPASSES AND MOUNTEBANKS

From 1500 on, the mountebanks, who for all of the medieval period had traveled the streets in Europe above all as individual artists, started to organize itinerant companies. The first associations could make use of the market squares, which in the meanwhile were established as important moments in the social life of that era. The fairs were reference points for traders of all sorts and as meeting and leisure time for the people who also came from the surrounding areas.

The life and the movements of the itinerant companies followed the cadence of the principle European fairs, such as Saint Laurent, Saint Germain and Saint Ovide in France, the Bartholomew fair in England and that which took place in front of the Kremlin in Russia.[11] In this context, there was a profitable approaching of different types, which gave life to a characterization of itself: the Theatre Foraine, of which, we can cite for example, Les Forces de l'Amor et de le Magie, an ensemble of acrobatics, rope dancers, juggling and theatre.[12]

The fairs were lively performance places filled with troubadour, street dancers, contortionists, tarot readers, elixir sellers, and jugglers who in the fair received a sort of recognition for their professionalism. Together with this they obtained not only the tolerance of the authorities but even perspectives, such as what happened in Nuremberg in 1680, when the city counselor paid a "ball master" to teach the young folk of the city to juggle and rope walk.

At this proposition, Strehly wrote that "the old juggling style, that which one still sees in the scenes of the second order or in the stands at the fairs, consisted in the art of throwing at times four or five brass balls." To juggle with balls remains in every era the ABC of jugglers—they are without doubt the most easily made objects. It is sufficient to roll up some rags, some string and there you have a low priced working prop, ideal for the penniless beginners.

Tightrope walkers remained, however, the central nucleus of the representations of the fair and many of them were also jugglers, among these the incomparable Dupuis, whose traces had even reached us, who, while in equilibrium on the rope, juggled with three apples that ended up spiked on two forks held in his hands with the third held between his teeth.

At the end of 1700 the Englishman Anthony Maddox juggled six balls while walking on a slack rope. (Ropewalkers can be divided into steel wire-walkers that performed at a medium height, rope-walkers at a great height and the virtuous "ropedancers" who carried out their exercises on a slack rope.)

ANTHONY MADDOX, ENGLAND 1753

JUGGLER PERFORMING AT BERLIN FAIR, 1830

---

1 Weber, Carl W., *Panem et Circenses*, Düsseldorf, EconVerlag, 1983, p. 217.

2 Sagemuller, Hermann, *Michael Kara—Konig der Jongleure, Jongleur der Konige*, Baldingen, Selbstverlag, 1973, p. 7.

3 Qifeng, Fu, *Chinese Acrobatics Through the Ages*, Beijing, Foreign Languages Press, 1985, pp. 7, 8.

4 Qifeng, Fu, op. cit., p. 8.

5 Definition of Menendez Pidal reported in Allegri, Luigi, *Teatro e spettacolo nel Medioevo*, Roma-Bari, Laterza, 1995, p. 62.

6 *Il Didascalion di Ugo di SanVittore*, Cfr. Allegri, op.cit., p. 68.

7 Ziethen, Karl-Heinz, 4000 *Years of Juggling*, Cauvigny, 1981, vol.I, p. 16.

8 Now conserved at the Nuremberg Museum, Germany; Ziethen, p. 16.

9 Qifeng, Fu, op. cit., p. 2.

10 For a deeper look into the intercultural exchanges between Asia and Europe view Savarese, Nicola, *Teatro e spettacolo fra Oriente e Occidente*, Roma-Bari, Laterza, 1992, p. 542.

11 Makarov, Serguey, *Russian Circus Through Ages*, Rosgoscirk, Moscow, 1996, p. 2.

12 Moudouès, Rose-Marie, *Il Teatro a Parigi*, Roma, Bulzoni, 1994, p. 127.

II

THE RING AND THE STAGE

CIRCUS AND VARIETY

In the second half of the 1700's, jugglers and mountebanks were able to find better jobs, compared to work found in the dusty streets, circus rings and variety theatre stages. The most important historians of juggling are in agreement that 1852 was the year that variety was born and its first appearance is usually considered the English Music Hall. That year the London entrepreneur, Charles Morton, opened Canterbury Hall, where amidst singing and dancing he inserted various artistic exhibitions. Actually in all of England, there had been for quite a while the so-called pleasure gardens—small bars immersed in parks—where one could sip a drink and avoid the hot summer, sheltered by the pergolas covered in ivy and other vegetation.

Already from 1683 one of these places had taken the name of Sadler's Wells Theatre and had started the custom of taking in mountebanks hired from the street. The man considered to be the first clown in history worked at Sadler's, a performer named Joseph Grimaldi, whose grandfather Giuseppe (or "Iron Legs") had clear Genovese origins. Following the example of the pleasure gardens, all the bars and even the crudest taverns had started hosting numbers of varying type and levels.

These performances enjoyed an always increasing number of visitors when, in 1737, the Licensing Act came out. The then-Prime Minister, Robert Walpole,

AMEDI NEWPORTE

in an attempt to limit the fashionable political satire, gave state powers to parliament to prohibit all theatre works that weren't expressly authorized by his office. This provoked a sharp fall for the theatre productions but, however, in that period the English theatre continued to exist thanks to the fame of actors such as Charles Macklin and David Garrick. The Licensing Act considerably limited the activities of the official theatres and lengthened the queues of spectators in the various amusement arcades, which, by then were annexed to any restaurant or even bowling alleys.

In France, even though for different reasons, there was a similar expansion. The origin can be traced back to June 8, 1670, the day that Louis XIV created an ordinance for the restoring and lengthening of the Avenue that went from the gates of Saint-Antoine up to the Rue de Filles-du-Calvaire, also meeting the gates of Saint-Martin. For nearly two centuries, it became the "Boulevard" for the Parisians. Along these streets all the mountebanks assembled who had abandoned the biggest fairs in the outskirts of Paris, which for one reason or another had fallen into disuse. The boulevard, anticipating by a couple of centuries the famous Broadway, quickly became a kind of showbiz neighborhood where myriad theatre and amusement arcades popped up of all sorts and where many of the most important actors of that era trained and worked.

The spontaneous reciprocal influence between the higher and lower arts became stronger than ever before. It became the norm that ropewalkers, acrobats and dancers worked together in the same shows. In 1814, Louis XVIII authorized the opening of the Theatre des Acrobates, in which the famous ropewalker Madame Saqui exhibited herself. Next to that, and following its huge success, the celebrated Theatre des Funamboles opened, where amongst others exhibiting themselves, were Frederick Lemaitre and Jean Gaspard Deburau— one of the greatest mime artists of all time destined to make known and appreciated the figure of Pierrot at the highest levels.

ROMEO CAPITE

Soon after, new buildings were built in the whole of Europe to be dedicated solely to entertainment purposes. In the meantime, however, they were changing their production systems, not based on companies but on individual artists signed up by directors and entrepreneurs. These theatres became generically known as variety theatres even if, according to their peculiarity or country of origin, they could have been called Variété, Ministrel, or Spezialitatentheater or, as we have already mentioned, Music Halls. It was in these halls, in the fifty years between the last two centuries, that jugglers found the most public and critical success they ever had.

Circus, on the other hand, was born in England around 1768 when an ex-lance corporal of the English Cavalry, Philip Astley, opened an equestrian amphitheatre, in which he showed equestrian handiness, virtuous acrobats and comical intervals. The enormous success of this new formula, in its various components thousands of years old, was owed to the new social conformation that the continent was assuming prior to the industrial revolution. For the masses of half-illiterate people who went from the countryside to the cities, a visual show was without doubt more adapt. On the other hand, the more appreciated form of theatre—the sentimental drama, spectacular action and the farce—were none other than a sort of circus adaptation of the traditional comedy and tragedy.[1]

ENGLISH CLOWN

The circus artist presented analogies with the actor of the "Commedia dell'Arte" being actor, author, register and showman at the same time. The juggler must practice, build a routine, position the exercises in such a way as to make his performance fluid, create a sort of plot for the act, taking into consideration the taste of the public and the tendencies of the time. He had to find the music to adapt to accompany the evolutions and design his own costumes in such a way as to satisfy the esthetical needs, as well as the realistic needs, taking into account the physical nature of his exhibition. However, while the theatre works as a means to augment the literacy to he who participates, the circus on the other hand, slows the education.

In any case, starting from the second half of the 1700's, with the birth of the circus and the codification of the variety theatres, and thanks to the greater quantity of existing material, one started to be able to distinguish between the different types of jugglers.

CLOWNS AND HORSE RIDERS

In the circus, always being a great place for jugglers, it assumed a role of grand importance for clowns and equestrian acrobats. The origin of the figure of the clown has for a long time been an object of study and one can trace back some of the characters in a few

BRIATORE BROTHERS

MASTER CHARLY JEE

Shakespearean comedies. It seems, however, out of discussion that the nation of origin may have been England and that in English the word "clown" means fool, particularly in a rural context. We have already mentioned the significant figure of Joseph Grimaldi, the father of clowning, of which Charles Dickens wrote *Le Memorie* and, even if he may have had Italian origins, made his fame in Great Britain, the country where circus was born and exhibited the first circus clowns.[2]

It is interesting to note that the first clowns in the circus were really artists who carried out their routine in a comic and amusing way. There were comic acrobats, comic horse riders and, consequently, comic jugglers. Only subsequently did the clown form his own category, becoming the pre-eminent symbol of the circus world. Many of the first clowns were, therefore, also expert jugglers.

Thomas Kemp, the Great Franconi of Cirque Olympique, balanced a spinning top and a peacock's feather on his chin. The German Jean-Baptiste Auriol, making his debut in 1834, was one of the greatest circus artists of all time—as important for the Germans as Jerome "Boum-Boum" Medrano was for the French; that is, a complete artist, able to perform in any discipline, always making it, however, humorous.

With the main contribution from the eclectic Americans, clowning transformed into eccentric comedy. Another important peculiarity of the circus was the connotations with the equestrian shows. It's interesting to note that, while the antique equestrian disciplines, like the medieval contests or the Chinese 100 Games, were carried out in elongated hippodromes to reach high speeds, the circus introduced the characteristic round ring. This shape allowed the best method to carry out juggling and acrobatic feats on horses, making use of the centripetal force released in the circular run of the animal, helping the artist to stay on his feet.

The equestrian juggler found his ideal collocation in the circus ring. An Englishman named Thomas Price, who exhibited himself as Philip Astley even as early as 1770—

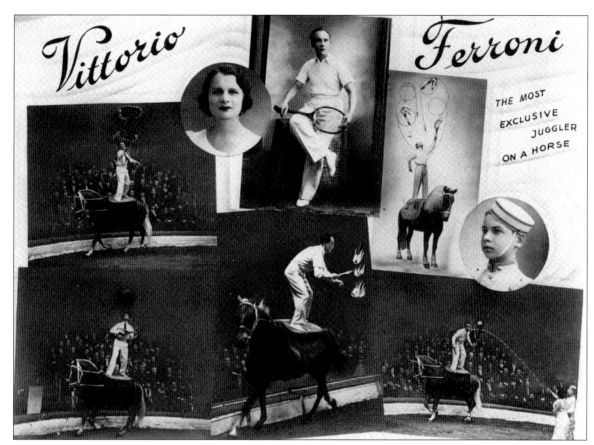

FERRONI

in the very first shows of the inventor of the circus—carried out exercises on a horse that consisted of spinning plates on the ends of wooden sticks held in his hands. More or less, in the same years, a Belgium man named Peter Mahveu was able to juggle three balls in the right hand while holding a plate in the other—all this standing up on a galloping horse. Peter Mahveu lived from 1765 to 1863 and was the first artist able to carry out these difficult exercises, even from the age of 16.[3]

Regarding the American circus, there are two artists who contend for the title of pioneer: John Bill Rickets and Thomas Pool. One thing is certain. Both were talented horseback jugglers able to seize oranges by piercing them with forks. In 1810, again in America, a Mr. Covetana juggled with rings, hats and gloves while standing on a horse. The famous German circus Renz in the first half of the 19th century boasted about having the excellent horseback juggler Lorenz Wulff, who specialized in throwing plates in circular trajectories that ended up returning to his hands. The same Renz circus confirmed itself as an important training place of sound artists hosting another good horseback juggler in their show, Gotthold Schumann, who worked together with his brother Albert.

Still at Renz, a few years later, the Briatore Brothers worked standing in a double column, on horseback, while one of them juggled with seven balls. Many circus ringmasters were also strong horseback jugglers. The Russian Nikolai Akimowitsch Nikitin, adopted son of one of the first ringmasters and Russian circus owners, was an elegant horseback juggler who later worked in a duet with his son, Nikolai Nikolajewitsch. After the First World War, the Nikitins assumed the management of many stable circuses situated in Moscow, Nishni Nowgorod, Kasan, Saratow and Zarizyn. In this way, having hosted many other strong jugglers, and observing them, they could refine their style and broaden their repertoire. Other important names were Artiselli and Williams, Charles Fillis, Charles Ducos, Cariot, Georg Burkhardt, Foottit, Master Charly Jee and Agnes Krembser, George Franz Sidoli, Thomas Belling (considered the inventor of the clown August) and Victor Riego, who standing up on his galloping horse could juggle with plates, balls and fire torches, all while playing his violin at the same time.

THE ORIENT AND ORIENTALISM

In 1862, the Baron George Eugene Haussmann, the then-Parisian prefect, planned on behalf of Napoleon III a new program to restore the French Capital. In his plan, there were many good points but, unfortunately, it had the downside of suppressing the Boulevard du Temple. It was the end of an era. Along the Boulevard were the greatest entertainment halls of that time. From the Franconi's Cirque Olimpique to Folies-Dramatique and, in the lively and busy avenue, one could meet all types of artists and fairground booths.[4] There was a saying, "When God is bored, he opens his windows to look at the Parisians' avenues." In England, just a few years earlier, in 1843, the Theatre Act came into being and gave the legitimate theatres the privilege of dialogue. The variety theatres after that made the final transformation towards mainly visual performances. In 1852, Charles Morton opened Canterbury Hall, giving definite guidelines to Music Hall and in 1890 opened the most luxurious of the Music Halls of that era—The Palace.

Soon after, true variety circuits were formed that gave an extraordinary vital impulse to all the acrobatic arts and forced the entrepreneurs to hunt for sensational attractions able to please the always-more demanding public. One of the most-followed trends was "orientalism."

MOOTY AND MEDUA SAME

ADVERTISEMENT, 1897

The search was always on to sign-up Asian artists who were able to satisfy the enormous demand. Furthermore, the not-so-good economic conditions in the eastern countries stimulated many artists to form companies and set off in adventurous tours in the wealthier countries of Europe, America and Southeast Asia. Whilst the majority of the European artists were only just having stages to work on, the Orientals, and particularly the Chinese, were already used to working in theatres and other places specially made for entertainment purposes.

In many large eastern cities, there were famous entertainment districts, where the public was offered all sorts of diversions, from exquisite cuisine to the shadow and marionette shows, and to gratification, often the most requested and appreciated, of any possible sexual desire. Even in these ambiguous performance places, the artists were obliged to present well-packaged routines and to constantly improve their performances. Juggling, therefore, had various developments that brought about the invention of new specialties.

For example, a routine called the "billiard head" where the artist wore a leather bowl on his head in which the wooden balls with which he juggled ended up. Another new number that had great success, was where strange objects like shuttlecocks, or duck feathers fixed to a bronze coin, were juggled with the feet. The form and weight of these objects was such that once thrown into the air they executed particular figures. In this

TAKASHIMA

discipline, much practiced in the second half of the 19th century, there was even a manual written by Xiang Ling Zhi Nan, *How to Shuttlecock Kick*, published towards the end of the 1800's and having numerous reprints.

However, the first Asian jugglers who obtained great success in the west were from India. According to an English manuscript written in 1819, an artist named Ramo Samee worked in Europe. He juggled with hollow brass balls the size of large oranges. Like many fellow countrymen that followed him, he was a sword-swallower. The first Asian jugglers to visit Berlin were, in 1823, the Mooty Brothers and Madame Same, who performed at the Jagorschen Halle under Unter den Linden, showing difficult pole swinging and complicated ball juggling. In Italy, around 1840, there appeared the Indian troupes from Ham Sing and Miss Odiska, both signed up to the Corini circus.

European travelers who had visited the Orient at the beginning of the 18th century often published diaries containing various details on the Asian world that inspired fairy tales. Here's how Karl von Holtei, in his novel *Die Vagabunden*, published in 1851, tells of an Indian juggler, Moti Sami. (Probably inspired by the already mentioned Mooty.)

"That which many considered a good artistic level was only a fifth of what Mooty Same was able to demonstrate. He spun rings with his big toes, with his thumbs he spun others in opposite directions, at the same time balancing a parasol on his forehead, and on the top, he filled empty bird shapes with peas blowing from a straw that he held between his lips. Unfortunately, when they tried to bring him to Europe, this extraordinary artist not being used to the rigid western climate, died with the melancholy of the thought of never seeing again the banks of his beloved river Ganges."[5]

What was there of a magical nature in the performance of an eastern artist beyond his talent? Strehly had already noticed: "A far eastern priest celebrating a Buddhist mass is no more solemn than a Japanese artist who prepares for his balances."[6] As a matter of fact, the learned physicality of the Asian artists assumed an almost mystical connotation when it became a way to enter into communication with something superior than the quotidian. Throughout the centuries, the Buddhist priests had popularized their religion through the performance of the 100 Games, in which acrobats and jugglers found themselves next to shamans revealing their pure bodily expression that, going beyond the quotidian, spoke with the "other side."[7] Read, for example how the Korean poet Choi Tchi-won, born in 857 AD, saw the exhibition of a juggler in the 100 Games:

"The body twisted, the arms shook; the spectators turned their gaze towards the moon and the stars. Even Seung Nyo (famous Chinese juggler) couldn't juggle better. What's more, the waves in the eastern sea were silent and held their breath to appreciate at best."[8]

The juggler became "juggler-shaman" and kept the ability to connect with the divine. The performance becomes an esthetical and mystic act becoming Zen. Like Zen, it is not good nor bad—the marvelous acrobatics aren't comprehensible in a moral way, neither in a positive nor negative way; and they are pure bodily expressions, detached from any daily context. The stage becomes a temple where one can celebrate, with no discrimination between religions—only maximum respect for what one is doing.

Thanks to similar descriptions and the first tours of the Asian artists, the collective imagination founded the conviction that the Orient was a type of juggler's paradise. The Spanish word *Malabarista* (juggler), comes from the Indian coastal region Malabar, and highlights how widespread this conviction may have been. Not only the spectators but also the western artists were amazed at the skill of their colleagues and above all of the sensations that they provoked. For this reason, they started to adopt the customs, ways, and names of the "Oriental look" and to even lie about their provenance in an attempt to sell themselves better.

One doesn't understand how these disguises, at times very badly made, could deceive the even naive public of that time. The terms Indian and Red Indian were often confused in bizarre concoctions. The famous Otti Motti, for example, passed himself off as an Indian horseback rider and the Italian Berra as a Red Indian illusionist, where the traditional origin was the exact opposite. Karl Rappo, who we will speak about later, was considered master of the Indian poles and the Red Indian Marobelli was really from Venice.

However, a strange fate befell the Indian artists. Around 1850, when the habit of signing up mainly Chinese and Japanese artists had stabilized, the Indians had completely disappeared. It is probable that the success of the troupes were in some way coupled to the fate of the Indian companies. The renowned commercial organization that enjoyed the monopolistic regime in nearly all of the Indian Territories ceased

KATSNOSHIN AWATA

their activity in 1858—the same period that the Indian jugglers ceased their European tours. The reason given was, however, different and more profound. It was seen that away from the European fashion of the moment, fickle as it was, the Indian juggler fell into a period of decline from which he was never to escape. The Indians' place was, therefore, taken by the far-eastern troupes, among which the more famous in the first years were from Japan: Kikuta, Misaka, Toyokochi, Yochitaro, Masungoro, Yamamoto and Kokota.

In 1832, the theatre in London's Drury Lane hosted Lau Laura, making her the first Chinese juggler to perform in Europe. Lau Laura formed part of the Arr-Hee acrobatic troupe. In 1866, a troupe of 24 people, captained by the Japanese Jean Torikata, came to Europe. Torikata was an ex-dentist who had decided to form his own company of acrobats, among which were many valid jugglers. The troop's debut was at London's Covent Garden and its success was such that they were invited to Windsor Castle, where they exhibited in private for the Royal Family. The troupe even carried out a tour in Italy where, however, following internal disputes, they divided, part of which formed a new troupe that reinforced the already existing Chinese troupe Ten-Arr-Heebe. On the other hand, all of these troupes had a particular characteristic in common, that is, they were subject to continual fission, fusion, cessation and rebirth.

The Japanese, Ja-En-See and Takashima, performed in England in 1867 in an act that contained exercises with a spinning top that spun in precarious equilibrium on strings and even on the border of a fan. The two Asians were also Chinese pole masters, who played with four woods at the same time and who anticipated previously unheard-of vertical moves. The most imitated of the Japanese artists was undoubtedly Katsnoshin Awata, who was also the court juggler of Mikado from Japan. Awata's most successful exercises were those in which he used a mouthstick that he held between his teeth and on which one or two balls of various dimensions were bounced. The possible combinations were more

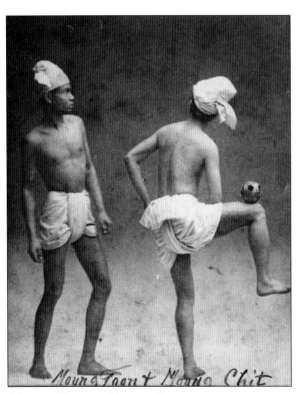

MOUNG TOON & MOUNG CHIT

or less unlimited and his skill could not be outclassed. Such exercises were by then known as Awata's Games and taken up by many western jugglers. In 1895, another exceptional Asiatic group performed in Europe, the Moung Toon Trio from Burma. This trio didn't use their hands, but passed glass and bamboo balls to each other using only their heads and feet.

The Asian mastery was owed to the fact that the artists from the ancient half-kingdom were able to pass on their own particular talent without problems. One reason was because they hadn't known the dark years of the medieval era and also because, as we have already mentioned, there had been proper performing arts schools constructed in the east, such as the already cited Gardens of Peri. Furthermore, these artists used props such as fans, large jars or Indian-rubber balls, whose mere presence sufficed to satisfy the public's exoticism.

The interesting amalgamation between the eastern and western arts continued. Little by little, as the new juggling styles arrived in Europe, the local artists took them on. Depending on their honesty, they behaved in two different ways: either "westernizing" the new styles and props or, as was often the case, making out that they were Asian. There were also those like the Londoner William Peppercorn d'Alvini, (1847-1891), who called themselves the Japanese of the Japanese. The fashion of the Asian troupes continued up until after World War I, when in Europe the Chinese troupes Riogoku, See-Hee-Hama-mura and Guo-Pao-Chi still performed. The Japanese troupes, the Family Sawade, Soga Trio, George-Wong troupe, Takahashi and Fuji-Akimoto, were also still operative. The skill of these artists continued to be outstanding. One component of the Japanese Okabe family was where they juggled with three balls in one hand while standing on the other—one of his colleagues was an antipodean who juggled with a barrel on his feet, a fan in one hand and five rings in the other. Takeo and Koma Namba, who performed in America, were both capable of juggling with four balls balanced head-to-head.

THE STANISLAVSKIJ METHOD

The success of the true Asian jugglers also came swiftly to Russia, a land where the circus and variety have always been loved. In those years, they could boast of numerous permanent circuses and variety theatres. Furthermore, many Russian intellectuals, who in the first decades of the 1800's changed the face of the theatre, were openly enthralled by the circus world. Stanislavskij, in his autobiography, wrote of having had his first rapport with performances, like many children of that time, through the magic of the circus ring, "the most beautiful place in the world," which made him decide to be a circus director when he grew up.[9] Other than loving the circus arts in general, it is interesting to note how Stanislavskij may have been in a special way astonished by some Japanese jugglers:

"For all winter our house changed into a Japanese corner. An entire family of Nippon acrobats, who worked in the local circus, were with us day and night. They taught us many Japanese customs: the way to walk, bend, dance, gesticulate. We learned how to juggle with fans, to throw them over the shoulder, under the leg and above all, we learned how to make all the poses in a way that every passage, note, and key may have had its corresponding action with the fan."[10]

Without wanting to go deeper into the complex discussions of Stanslavskij's Method, we can underline how all the Asian artists of that time were able to incite in the public, crude or sophisticated that they may have been, something more than simple wonder for their expertise. Something that the great director had been able to appreciate in the actors, Hanako and Mei Lanfang.[11] Stanislavskij was very taken aback by the artist to the point of using him as a stimulus to the actors in his lessons:

"Observe the circus equilibrist: holding a staff on his forehead, a plate on the staff, a sphere on the plate. His attention is turned to every one of these objects. In the same way you must train your attention on the various levels."[12]

THE CULT OF THE FARCE AND OF THE WEIRD

In the first half of the 1900's, all the disciplines that had dragged themselves around the medieval fairs continued their travels with the circuses and the stages of the variety theatres. Among the various types of juggling that developed in those years, one had particular success—the strongman juggling. This united the juggling of heavy objects with virtuous "Herculean" physiques. The demonstrations of strength were to all effects among the oldest forms of entertainment, even if they could not always be categorized with the various juggling types. They were often included within fight meets that were more, often than not, staged. Perhaps it was also for this anciently known rigging that strongman juggling has always had certain skepticism about it. For the public it was, in fact, difficult to appreciate the weight of the objects that were used during the performances and consequently the level of difficulty.

Among those artists who performed in this promiscuous genre, and the first to win certain notoriety, was Karl von Rapp, who was born in Innsbruck on May 14, 1800, in a high-ranking family. Already at the age of 19, von Rapp was a strong athlete with a powerful physique. Fascinated by the performance of a so-called "Indian" juggling company that had performed in his city, he decided to pursue them, against the will of his rich family that had always been opposed to that way of life. His juggling apprenticeship was not one of the easiest.

Determined to make a name for himself in the performing world, von Rapp spent the first few years of his career performing in the squares and markets with two large, trained dogs. Subsequently, he decided to make the most out his gigantic physique, performing as Hercules under the pseudonym of Karl Rappo. In 1828, he chose to appear as an Indian juggler. After which he decided that his specialty would be that of strongman juggler. At the Cristoph de Bach circus, for example, he already handled six steel balls and bent large iron bars. He still didn't perform a well-defined activity. For a certain period of time, he was often hired by an important circus and for other times he would perform on his own

KARL RAPPO

in fairs and markets, like his predecessors had done for centuries. This way of working was typical of what was happening in those years.

Many artists, having finally left the long anonymity in which they had been forced, weren't able to insert themselves into a better-structured system because this system wasn't altogether formed yet. To remedy these inconveniences, derived from this precarious situation, Rappo decided to form a small versatile company that gave him certain autonomy and the possibility to perform independently from the whims and the needs of the market and of the contractors. The company, called Rappo Theatre, was made up, other than himself and his close friends, of some novices. One of these, Karl Johann Schaeffer, was destined in a few years to become the founder of a large dynasty of artists.

Arriving at a certain success, the Rappo Theatre was able to perform in Berlin, Paris, and London, which were beginning to be known as the "capitals of the show business world." The repertory of the Rappo Theatre was vast enough to allow Rappo to fill a vari-

PAULA AND ELSA DE LUCA

ety show in three parts on its own. In the first part, all of the components of the troupe performed various Chinese and Arabic exercises that followed the trends of the era and complicated Icarian tricks. (The specialty of the Icarians was a variation of the antipodean, invented by one Richard Risley Carlisle, who had had the idea of substituting the objects normally juggled by the feet, with his own children, such that for many years this discipline was called "Risley's Games"). In the second part, Rappo himself juggled with heavy objects, like differently weighted cannon balls that he threw in the air to catch on his back, to then roll from one hand to the other. In the third part, that closed the show, Rappo presented himself in a military outfit, starting thereafter a tradition destined to have many imitators.

Rappo performed a series of incredible exercises that contributed to reinforce his fame. In one of these, he balanced an iron anchor of real dimensions on his chin, on top of which was placed a cannon ball. The grand finale was amazingly pyrotechnic: he placed on his head a model of a battleship with many cannons and flags, he then started to walk backwards and forwards to show everything to the public until ultimately, at his order, the miniature pieces of artillery opened fire with splendidly colored Bengal lights. In this way, he preceded by a century the illusionist Harry Houdini, who used to attract the attention of the mass media by chaining and hanging himself from poles on skyscrapers at dizzying heights.[13]

Rappo had demonstrated his strength in his performances by attaching himself to a blade of a Dutch windmill, holding a carriage with eight men and a horse on his shoulders and by freeing a carriage in Berlin that had a wheel caught in a crack in the road.[14] On that occasion, he simply bent under it and lifted it out. Prince Karl, who was looking out of the window of the Royal Palace at that moment, appreciated this feat. Full of admiration and respect for Rappo, the prince wanted to invite the artist to one of his receptions. It was the custom of the day that every extravagant individual in the country came to visit the Court.

Karl Rappo found his distinct blessing in Russia, one of the countries where, at that time, such performance forms were most appreciated. In Moscow, where he finally settled, he performed in front of Czar Nicola I from Romanov, whom he found friendly and whom had often wanted Rappo as a guest at his Court. In the Russian capital, Rappo also met his death. He contracted typhoid and died in 1854. The strongman juggling didn't disappear however. At that time, one could find true athletes who used their physical force to make their performances more impressive, on every variety theatre's stage and in every circus ring.

The strong jugglers weren't only men—there were also examples of the female strong jugglers, too. The simple fact that they were women performing in this discipline was enough reason to increase the curiosity. Among the first artists to exhibit in this discipline, from 1830 onwards, we can remember the German Elisa Sarafin Luftmann, and the Frenchwoman Anita Schaeffer (from the famous dynasty), the Italian De Luca Sisters and, above all a few years later, Miss Atleta. An incredibly powerful artist, Miss Atleta, born in 1868, called herself the strongest woman in the world and was able to juggle with steel balls that weighed 44 pounds each. Not only that, but she was also able to hold, on her stomach, a pole on which two horses were attached. The Russian Katchen "Sandwina" Brumbach, born in 1884, had inherited her strength from her father, Philipp Brumbach, who in his youth was a Russian weightlifting champion. Sandwina juggled balls weighing between 33-44 pounds that she threw and caught behind her neck. Lying down on a stool, she held a trestle on her stomach on which 16 men walked

CLAUDIA ALBA

EMIL NAUCKE

all at the same time! Other women to perform in "power juggling" were Victoria
Kanonenkonigin and Claudia Alba, who performed various difficult tricks of equilibrium,
strength and juggling.

The strongmen jugglers were an example of how, in those years, beyond the power of
the muscles, the perfection of the body was appreciated, giving merit, perhaps, to the
spread of the statuesque and classic forms. Paradoxically, next to the cult of the force and
of physical perfection, the performances of the "freaks" had a great success, i.e., all those
individuals who had bizarre bodily anomalies.[15]

The most famous manager of these stupendous menageries was the great Phineas Taylor
Barnum, a person of versatile character and of the quick bluff, who had even built a building
in New York under the pompous name of the American National Museum, exhibiting every
type of extravagance possible and imaginable.[16] It was also thanks to this consolidated
public taste for the bizarre in that era that the German Emil Naucke obtained certain notoriety. Naucke, born in 1855, in Mecklenburg, performed strongman juggling but was
appreciated above all else for being one of the Kolossalmenschen, or Giants, the names

which men of these immense proportions were called. At 18 years of age, he had already reached what would be his cresting weight for the rest of his life. He weighed 470 pounds.

Naucke dedicated himself at free fighting and there wasn't an adversary able to beat him. No one could embrace his almost six-foot circumference. He was wider than tall. This enormous volume was not all flour in a sack—he was in fact an actor's son, having inherited the predisposition to obesity from his mother's father, Schmied, who in his youth would have outdone Naucke by reaching 518 pounds. Naucke not only exhibited his enormousness; but he was also a valiant and versatile artist, acrobat, cyclist, comedian and juggler. He was able to juggle three swords and two heavy iron balls at the same time. Lying on his back, as an antipodean, he spun two small handlebars with his hands and a larger one with his feet. He reached such notoriety that, at his death in 1900, the term "Naucke" remained for many years synonymous with an overweight person.

FRANK EDERS

---

1   Medolesi in Meldolesi—Taviani, *Teatro e spettacolo nel primo Ottocento*, Roma-Bari, Laterza, 1991, p.181.

2   Dickens, Charles, *L'anima del Circo*, Udine, Trapezio, 1989, p. 617.

3   Culhane, John, *The American Circus: An Illustrated History*, New York, Henry Holt, 1990, p. 504.

4   The atmosphere that lightened the Boulevard was partly reconstructed in the 1945 film *Les Enfants des Paradis* with the screenplay by Jaques Prevert directed by Marcel Carné, with the participation of Etienne Decroux.

5   Ziethen, Karl-Heinz, *Die Kunst der Jonglerie*, Berlin, Henschlverlag, 1988, p. 14.

6   Strehly, George, *L'Acrobatie et les acrobats*, Paris, S. Zlatin, 1903, p. 206.

7   Ottaviani, Gioia, *L'attore e lo sciamano*, Roma, Bulzoni, 1984.

8   Da Pyong-hi Chong, *Danses masquées et jeux de marionettes en Corêe*, Paris, POF 1975, Ottaviani, Gioia.

9   Autobiography p. 16, here by Malcovati, Malcovati, Fausto, *Stanislavskij. Vita, opere e metodo*, Roma-Bari, 1988, p. 4.

10 Autobiography pp. 80-81, here by Malcovati, op. cit. p. 8.

11 Hanako was an appreciated Japanese actress who revived the magnificence of Sada Yacco. Mei Lanfang was one of the principle interpreters of the Theatre of Peking, specializing in feminine roles.

12 Cited in *Stanislavskij riformatore dell'arte operistica*, Moskva 1983, p. 342, here by Malcovati, op. cit., p. 109.

13 Gresham, William Lindsay, *The Man Who Walked Through Walls*, London, Victor Gollancz, 1960, p. 306.

14 Groth, Lothar, *Die starken Manner, Eine Geschichte der Kraftakrobatik*, Berlin, Henschelverlag, 1985.

15 Browning, Todd, 1932, *Freaks*.

16 Harris, Neil, *Humbug, The Art of P.T.Barnum*, Chicago-London, The University of Chicago Press, 1973, p. 337; Saxon, A.H., *P.T.Barnum, The Legend and The Man*, New York/Oxford, Columbia University Press, 1989, p. 437.

III

THE REASONS FOR THE FORMALITY

ACROBATIC DRAMATIZATION

The "variety" theatre was becoming the pre-eminent show in the growing middle-class. The most appreciated halls were, in fact, positioned in the center of the city, tastefully furnished and frequented above all by those of the upper class. The props and the artists' costumes changed with the public trends. In addition to military uniforms, sporting outfits and especially elegant evening-wear also appeared. Together with this, the use of scenery and stage props started to spread.

The costumes of some jugglers gave them a hint of distinction (soldier, gladiator, etc.) that permitted them, in some way, to justify their strange goings on, on the stage. On the other hand, within the variety circuits the traditional structure of the act, that is a mere series of exercises carried out one after the other with no apparent logical connection other than that of the increasing difficulty, didn't seem enough anymore to satisfy the public's needs. The public preferred performances with a plot or, at least, the appearance of a connecting thread such that, in those years, the theatre shows were born and established themselves.

Even in the circuses, the performances that had the greatest success in that era were those huge horseplays that re-enacted historical events. Some acrobats and jugglers decided to change the presentation of their numbers, in the hope of

AGOUST

PEREZOFF TROUPE

having more success, making smaller acts where the artist didn't act out himself but was also a character. Furthermore, this gave them the possibility to change their performance during their career, inventing different schemes in which to insert the same somersaults and juggling. The acts in this way assumed a narrative scheme, an internal fable, with a beginning, middle and end.[1]

Among such acts, one of the best loved was that of the restaurant juggler. The routine was so called because the props and the scenery used were clearly inspired by that of a restaurant. The inventor of this genus was the Frenchman Agoust in the second half of the 1900's. At the beginning of his career, even he had to earn his living in the squares. He was specialized in pole manipulations.

The "batonniste" presented an original exercise that consisted of throwing a dozen rings of differing dimensions in the air, which he caught at various heights on a type of elongated cone, a pointed stick that he had tied to his head. The sticks were then used in a thousand other ways. Thrown in the air like Chinese tridents or used to knock down objects placed in equilibrium on the nose of a spectator, Agoust was able to get into the variety theatres only after having perfected his act, adding some asymmetric juggling exercises that he carried out with various props, with different sizes and weights, such as throwing a steel flask in the air, a balled-up piece of paper and a bottle. Agoust performed in an elegant silk outfit with golden tassels and, as well as described above, juggled with oranges and porcelain plates. The latter were thrown so high that they nearly touched the ceiling in the hall.

However, his true success came when, around 1860, he was hired by the Hanlon-Lees troupe, already celebrated eccentric acrobats, to act out the part in a vaudeville show titled *Le Voyage en Suisse*, written by Raoul Tochè and Ernest Blum. Agoust was involved in a scene called La table d'hôtel, which was the most appreciated by the public, where the juggler sat at the table in a restaurant, in front, on a tiresome table-companion who wouldn't stop speaking. Agoust reacted by starting to juggle with the objects placed on the table until he inspired his companion, who also started to juggle with the tableware. Here is how the famous Theodore de Banville described the show:

"Blum and Tochè having had the art and the fortune to write an insane, overwhelming comedy written in prose that does leaps and somersaults mixed with lively rhymes that ring like a large number of bells swinging in a strong wind.[2] Within moments, all the items that lay on the table have become juggling balls without head or tail, rising, falling, rising again, remaining suspended in the air, darkening the sky, similar to waves whose fluxes my be able to hunt out the vague highs of deliria and of love."[3]

When he left the Hanlon-Lees troupe, Agoust decided to duplicate that scene, transforming it into a true attraction adapted for the circus and variety. He then created the routine, giving it a new life, which he called Un Restaurant Parisian. Agoust played an elegant Signor who, rather tipsy, made his entrance on stage with the help of a young, attractive lady. The scenery depicted a restaurant, in which they were greeted with respect by two other characters in the act, the waiter and the maitre d´. These started to lay the table in a frenetic and clumsy way; and Agoust, contaminated by this frenzy, took every object and threw them in the air or at the other companions always in increasingly comic and spectacular fashion.

In the end, when the table was perfectly laid, Agoust took the tablecloth in both hands, tugging it decisively towards him— while all the others present threw themselves forward in an attempt to save the porcelain. All their moves were, however, unnecessary, as the porcelain had remained firmly where they had stood upon the naked surface of the table. The exercises carried out in this number weren't

RAMBLER COMPANIE

extraordinary from the technical point of view but the whole scene was well devised and of a comical outcome.

Agoust had such success that he was able to perform in front of the tougher audiences at the more demanding venues, such as the Casino de Paris and the Cirque Napoleon, where shows were always of an extremely high level and where the famous Leotard, inventor of the trapeze, also worked. The Parisian restaurant routine had numerous copies. Among these, the Prince had particular success with a variation called La Cuisine Musical, in which he threw kitchen utensils and musical instruments that were being played, at the same time, by components of the troupe.

The group who took the restaurant juggling to the highest splendor was that of the Spanish performer, Perezoff. Their founder and leader, Charles Perez, was a valid artist who had already obtained a certain notoriety in England and was able to juggle up to seven balls, balancing a top hat on his forehead at the same time. Signing up another four artists he created Un Souper Animé Chez Maximís. The vast scenery comprised the entrance of a restaurant, a room with tables and a kitchen. The group arrived with up to 14 people and old and fascinating illustrations still exist showing these well-dressed artists throwing myriad sorts of objects.

PAUL CINQUEVALLI, THE STAR SYSTEM

In the second half of the 19th century, when cinema and television did not exist, the main entertainment for spectators of the western world was the variety theatre. Every large city had at least one hall dedicated to this activity. Vienna had three, Paris 11, Berlin and London 27. In Rome, there were the Salone Margherita, the Eden and the Olimpia. They were popular during the years when the variety artists were finally accepted by society and there was soon a structure created that denoted the acceptance of a true and orderly profession.

Syndicates and associations of class were born; and calendars and magazines dedicated to circus and variety were printed. In London, even a newspaper, *The Era*, which appealed to a mixture of performers and spectators alike, had the same distribution as the major daily English newspapers. Thanks to these particularly influential means of communication, and the impression that they gave to the collective imagination, it was possible for the artists to emerge and to be acclaimed by the public.

The first juggler to rise to be an international star of the variety show was the German, Paul Cinquevalli. His stage name was Paul Braun-Lehmann and he was born on June 14, 1859, in Lissa. From a young age, he showed a predisposition for gymnastics and acrobatics. At just six, he won numerous city and country gymnastic competitions. The Italian artist, Giuseppe Chiesi-Cinquevalli, director of a troupe of acrobatics and part of the renowned clown trio Chiesi-Bellon-Cinquevalli, incidentally while at Lissa, noted the fine physical appearance and Paul's enthusiasm and asked him to become part of his complex. Against his parent's will, Paul left home to start a long apprenticeship that would make him a great juggler. Thanks to his physique, Paul was able to work well in disciplines such as acrobatics, ropewalking and the trapeze.

The safety measures in those days for the artists who worked at great heights was virtually non-existent and in 1876, Paul fell from a height of 60 feet, breaking both his legs and almost all his ribs. After eight long months in bed, he decided to never again try these dangerous numbers and chose to excel in juggling. In tribute to his great master, when he debuted as a solo juggler in London's Covent Garden, he adopted the name Paul Cinquevalli and worked exclusively in variety theatres able to offer a high income.

In those days, the jugglers exhibited themselves in extremely decorated costumes and with props made especially for their acts. Paul's first innovation was using everyday

PAUL CINQUEVALLI

objects so that the public, knowing the weights and measures, could appreciate his exhibition better. Like many artists of that era, he wore tights with gold fringes that made his perfect proportions stand out. He was considered the king of symmetric juggling and was able to use every potential of his body, presenting routines never seen before and which were rarely repeated thereafter.

One of these was the "human billiard table," in which Paul threw billiard balls into the air that landed in little bags that he wore on his costume. The number was made more complicated when Cinquevalli struck the balls into the pockets with the cue, using his own back as a smooth green cloth. In another exercise, he held two billiard balls, in equilibrium one on top of the other, on the top of a cue placed on another ball placed inside a glass goblet whose base he held between his teeth!

Cinquevalli included fast somersaults and flic-flacs in between his juggling, which made his act fast and lively. He is given credit for the invention of the trick of "the cup on the head" that consisted of throwing a cup from the tips of his toes and catching it on the

PAUL CINQUEVALLI, POSTER 1905

head. The exercise is usually repeated until there is a tall pile of cups balanced on the head.

Another of his creations was that of throwing plates, like boomerangs, at an oblique angle in a way that they returned to his hands after having traveled a great distance. Cinquevalli didn't leave out of his act comic components like when, for example, he held a bottle full of water on top of a closed umbrella that poured out while he opened the umbrella without him, however, getting wet.

He continued furthermore to keep alive the tradition of the strongmen jugglers giving demonstrations of notable physical strength, for example, lifting three heavy wooden barrels or, even more spectacularly, holding a table between his teeth (while juggling three steel balls) on which his assistant pretended she was sleeping. Paul married the equestrian, Adeline Price, and in 1893, took English citizenship and settled down in London where, in 1912, he had the honor of participating in the first edition of the Royal Command Performance— a special gala evening put together especially for the English Royals.

Thanks to the strategy of using everyday leisure objects, such as billiards and tables, Cinquevalli won the sympathy of the emerging working classes. The upper classes preferred to crowd the variety halls, leaving the less-rich classes to frequent the itinerant circuses, while the aristocrats preferred the lyric operas or, anyway, the more "serious" shows. Thanks also to the arrival of easy communications and to the frenetic theatrical agencies, his fame crossed the ocean and he was soon invited to exhibit in Australia and, more than once, in America.

The situation for the variety theatres in America in the early 1920's was complicated. Glynne Wickham, in his *The History of Theatre*, wrote that such halls "offered at low cost shows put together quickly but, nevertheless, flowing for the tired workers at the end of a working day, putting at their disposal alcoholic drinks and feminine company in the passageway at the rear of the auditorium."[4]

This was true up until the last decades of the 1900's, that is until the manager, Tony Pastor, had in mind to create a clean-variety, cleaning from shows and theatrical buildings every hint of sex and any other unnecessary debauchery. From then on, mixed audiences were formed, an essential foundation on which to build the grand fortune of the variety show. With the puritanical adjustments, the halls reopened to all, such that it became a habit for the women to go to the variety on their own or with their young children. Only in this way could the variety widen its body of users and become, practically, the first mass media of the industrial age, capable of adopting a commercial organization adapted for modern times.

The managerial mechanism in America was more coherent than elsewhere and the "enrollment" system involved four different workers: the artist; the agent; the person in charge of the circuit; and the person in charge of the theatre. The artist was responsible for the goods; the agent—the seller; the person in charge of the circuit—the mediator; the manager of the theatre—the retail trader. Confidence was forged with this system, which entirely controlled the immense American market.

The more important circuits were the Proctor, Moss and the Keith-Albee, the latter, in particular, was the most powerful and managed over 700 theatres at the time of maximum expansion.[5] Furthermore in 1900, Keith and Albee, together with other hall owners, had already created the United Booking Office, a type of exclusive agency that checked all hiring at the vaudeville, taking a part of the percentages normally destined to the agents. The artists opposed this, forming the White Rats, a sort of syndicate that defended them against wrongdoing imposed by the trust.[6] Given that a major portion of the artists supporting the White Rats were America nationals, one may believe that a sort of self-independence may have favored them. On the contrary, the trust actually gave privilege to the foreign artists who may have given them less trouble.

Herbert Marinelli, like all the agents who worked for themselves, had had problems with the United Booking Office but this didn't impede the employment of the Italian Enrico Rastelli for a contract in the Keith-Albee circuit. From a few clauses inserted in the script, we can however understand what sort of tensions there were: it was written that in

CLARA BRAATZ

the Proctor, Moss and Keith it was understood that it was a unique chain and it was not allowed to perform in any city where there was a theatre of such a trust, neither live, nor via radio.[7]

It was the time of the Marx Brothers and many artists didn't act anywhere but in their own creations. This is why the circuit owners wanted to safeguard the radio transmissions that were all the rage then as well. Later, such rights protection was also extended to the cinematic projections. The monopolist regime seemed clear. As a matter of fact, while in Europe, Cinquevalli maintained his contact with numerous agents or even drew up his own contracts. In America, he worked only and always with the Keith-Albee circuit. Another strong clause in the contract was one, which permitted the director of the circuit to impose changes, or cuts in the artist's number to make sure that the performance maintained a clean nature and could be broadcast to the widest possible public audience.

On the other hand, the public of the variety theatres was greater in America than in any other part of the world and such an art form had almost become an institution. Even United States President Woodrow Wilson, in 1915, had to declare: "When I want to relax I enjoy watching a good variety show. If one sees a bad act you can be reasonably sure that the next will be better; while in a bad theatrical work there is no escape."[8]

It was in the United States that there were more variety theatres per head than anywhere else. One went to the "continuous," where the cheaper artists alternated themselves for the whole day, to the "Big-Time," the desired destination of any artist, with programmed performances, reserved places and super-paid stars. The public's taste came to influence not only the composition of the shows but also the very architecture of the theatrical buildings. They became a sort of profane cathedral, exceptional entertainment and meeting places. There was a saying at the time: "The show starts on the sidewalk." And indeed, while the traveling circus automatically created its own architecture, which had to be parceled up and moved quickly from place to place, the variety theatres were inserted instead into the urban development plans in small and large cities.[9]

To have wanted the figure of Cinquevalli to embody the juggler demonstrates once more what notoriety and consideration the celebrated artist may have attained. Such fame, however, ended fatally for him. After the start of World War I, the public and the London critics, who up until a few months beforehand had worshipped Cinquevalli, now, remembering his German origins, didn't pass up the occasion to challenge him. In those years, the foreign artists were welcomed as long as they came from friendly countries.

In this climate of sudden hostility, Cinquevalli hastened to tell everyone that he had naturalized his British citizenship many years earlier and that he had even had the honor of exhibiting in front of the Royal Family. This wasn't, however, enough to calm the hateful sentiments towards the artist. He felt devastated by this behavior, which was like an unexplained betrayal. In 1918, following great unhappiness, he died of heartbreak, although only a few years later his memory was fully revived. The career of Cinquevalli demonstrates how, between the two centuries, a juggling talent may have been able to attract public opinion and the attention of refined showmen, giving the figure of a juggler artistic dignity never to be known again.

Among his many merits, Cinquevalli also had that of stimulating feminine juggling. In 1890, Florrie Rhodesia was called, for example, the "Feminine Cinquevalli." However, the best female juggler of the time was Selma Braatz, born in 1855 in Berlin, and she was taught by her aunt Clara—famous for her act of soap bubbles full of cigarette smoke. She was the first woman to carry out a number in a purely masculine style. She knew how to juggle three tennis balls in her right and two in her left, then cross five with both hands and then even six—she was also a prodigy at the Awata Games.

NATIONALISM AND JUGGLING

The tendency to make even the variety and circus shows political was widespread. At the Franconi's Cirque Olimpique, one of the most famous permanent circuses of all time, there were historical, military horseback shows where Napoleon appeared as hero of the show. Other titles: Les Pages de l' Empereur; Le Prince Eugène et l'Imperatrice Josephine; Austerlizt; Schoenbrunn et Sainte Helène, up until a Passage du Mont Saint Bernard, "Military Glory in Seven Cadres."[10]

Even the jugglers adapted to this style and the strong-men jugglers, seen in their powerful characteristic, often motivated patriotic pride, were used for political propaganda. It was because of this that the artists, then engaged in this type of style, decided to wear military uniforms and had their major success in the years preceding World War I. Besides this "juggling militarization," it wasn't anything but the inverse of that which happened in China a couple thousand years earlier. In that far off country, the warriors dressed as artists, providing juggling with the first rudimental props that now—more modern and lethal—were once again given to the jugglers who dressed as warriors.

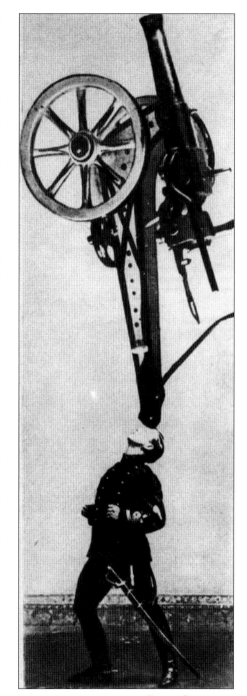

PAUL CONCHAS

An exemplary case of this was the Berliner Paul Conchas (whose real name was Paul Hutt) who chose the military uniform of a senior officer for his costume. He was assisted by a colleague, Julius Neumann, who was trusted with the comic part and was dressed as a rifleman. At the famous Wintergarten in Berlin, Conchas made his entrance into the scene accompanied by the music of the hymn Gloria Prussiana.

The exercises that he carried out were all of great difficulty, in keeping with the outfit that he had chosen. He juggled with three rifles and a cannon ball or balanced a cannon, with carriage and wheels, on his forehead. At a certain point in the performance, his partner, Julius Neuman, who wanted to take a well-earned break, sat down to eat something but was immediately lifted up, together with the table, chair and plates in one piece and Conchas held it all in equilibrium on his forehead.

On tour in America, Conchas was introduced as the strongest German soldier of all and his success was such that he was invited by John Rockerfeller to take part in a special show, which took place at the Palace of New York. His juggling was powerful and graceful, like when he took out from his pockets a handful of small objects that he quickly threw in the air. The first to come down was a mouthstick, which he caught between his teeth, then a cigar that he trapped in the right place, then a coin that he caught as a monocle and, finally, a burning match with which he lit a cigar. The major successes continued to happen in the United States where, after his death (which occurred in the middle of a tour in 1916), a funeral service was dedicated to him that had never been seen before for a German artist who had died overseas.

PAUL SPADONI

THE ELEGANCE OF THE ITALIAN NAMES

The upcoming middle-class had become one of the main reasons for the existence of the variety show and in every medium-sized city there was at least one place dedicated to that sort of entertainment. Jugglers, therefore, had to be able to imagine and, if possible, satisfy the expectations of that type of public. Among these there was the "elegance," an elastic and malleable conception that mutated according to the geographic and climatic locations. However, between 1700 and 1800, it was in some way defined and often associated with the Italian.

Passing the wave of Orientalism, which had driven many European artists to assume Asiatic nicknames, there then appeared a sort of Italian exoticism. Moreover, the Italian names had become famous in the European show business world, becoming a mark of refinement and elegance. From 1600, the prestigious technical scenes and lyrical opera names (such as Buontalenti, Bernini or Torelli for the first and Monteverdi for the second), or even the various Chiarini, began spreading out in the fairs of the whole continent.

The Franconi, Guerra and Ciniselli, among the colonies of the circus Nicoletti (initiator of the show of various arts), or the actors of the Commedia del'Arte and of the Comédie Italienne (Luigi Riccoboni, Carlo Bertinazzi or the Sticotti), all had a fascinating and magnetic influence over the spectators, not only due to the subtle heroism or to the elegance of their movements, but also due to their romantic and troubled private affairs.[11] For this reason, the circus artists often adopted Italian stage names.

SALERNO

One of the first jugglers to use an Italian stage name was Paul Krausse, known as Paul Spadoni, born in 1870 in Berlin. From his first meeting with the great juggler, John Holtrum, Paul had had the idea to carry out exercises with large cannon balls and to perform wearing a primitive costume, which would bring out the best of his Herculean physique. Eventually, Paul found his own direction thanks to the suggestions of another great juggler, Agoust, adopting the elegant stage name, Spadoni, giving him a certain exotic charm. Around 1893, having obtained masterful skills, Paul, together with his sister Agnes, created an act of Jongleur Moderne, in which both performers wore elegant evening wear and executed notable exercises.

KARA

Paul, for example, held his sister above his head with one hand and, with the other, juggled three large iron balls. While he spun a tureen on a pole with his left hand, he juggled three plates with his right with a ladder leaning against his shoulders on whose rungs Agnes climbed. The spectators appreciated these strange combinations and above all started to see characters in scenes with clothes not so dissimilar from theirs and with an almost mundane behavior. This increased their amazement for the contrast that was borne between the habitual and the extraordinary.

THE GENTLEMAN JUGGLERS

Spadoni was among the first to realize the importance of the elegant form that was always clearly revealed in contrast to that of the brute force. Kara completed such an evolved course and made famous the genus of the "gentleman juggler." Kara's real name was Michael Steiner and he was born on January 31, 1867, in Nuremberg. Like many predecessors, he did not come from an acting family—but had decided to leave home to follow his vocation. In the first years of his career, he performed in small circuses, thinking, above all, always of his training. He quickly carried out exercises of rare technical depth, such as juggling four balls in one hand, a movement not often equaled.

From the start, his style was very traditional but, one day, when he was contracted at the Circus Diaz in Lisbon, he was able to watch an artist who, behind stage, juggled with a walking stick, hat and cigar. In this way, he got the idea of transforming himself into a gentleman juggler and to take on a second stage name— this time, The Italian of Corradini. He began to get well known in the circus world and an agent, Franz Pospischil, called and suggested he go to the variety theatres and adopt a shorter and easier name to remember.

His growing success convinced the American manager, J. Hopkins, to hire him for a three-year tour in the United States. During his second year in the American contract, Kara had the occasion to watch a performance of a Japanese juggler, Satsuma, who performed the famous Awata Games. Kara was fascinated by the exercises in which the balls seemed to be "alive" and slid up and down the sticks that the Oriental artist held between his teeth. He attempted this and, discovering a certain talent, decided to divide his act in three parts: in the first he performed as a gentleman; in the second he wore the classic tasseled tights and executed the complicated Awata Games; in the third he presented foot-juggling tricks similar to the Burmese trio, Moung Toon.

He performed this act in 1894 at the Alhambra in London, and thereafter all the great variety theatres of Europe competed to have him on their bill. In 1908, he decided that his act could be based exclusively on the part that got the most success, that of the juggling gentleman, and for this reason, this portion of his performance was perfected even more. The scenery that he had adopted was composed of the inside of a caffè with a billiard room annexed. In an evening suit, with white velvet gloves, a top hat, walking stick and monocular, Kara, with magnetic appeal, made his entrance on stage and carried out his various exercises with an air of indifference that gave his performance a light, ironic touch.

The act was a flowing of movements without interruption and without losing an instant. Technically, his exercises were impeccable. For example, he held a billiard cue balanced on his forehead, made it slide down his back and caught it with his heel before it could touch the floor. He hadn't only established the genus of the gentleman, but had also used new props with inventive exercises. On top of a pole, about three feet long, he held a wooden panel with diagonal sleepers that functioned as corridors for the balls, which were thrown up there, and which rolled in this way from one place to another.

Kara also had big problems at the start of World War I, problems similar to those that had happened to Cinquevalli and nearly caused him to abandon

ADANOS

JETON

his livelihood. In August of 1914, during a performance in Paris, Kara was placed under arrest—as he was considered a revolutionary due to his German nationality. He was detained in various French prison camps until August of 1918, when he was finally released and given his freedom. Four years without training and practice may have ended the career of many a juggler. What was worse, all his props were lost. One of the most prepared jugglers, Adolf Salerno (another Italian stage name), came to help by lending Kara his props.

Kara began to train once again and, in late-1920, at the respectable age of 50, he obtained a contract for a five-year tour in the United States. It is probable that on that occasion he may have seen or heard of Enrico Rastelli, who had great success in performing at the Palace in New York in 1923. In 1929, at the age of nearly 60, Kara said good-bye to his career—performing for the last time at the Scala in Berlin. He died 10 years later in a town close to München, where he had settled down.

During this time, the genus of the gentleman juggler enjoyed great success and there were many who carried on the tradition. Other notable "elegant" jugglers were Bellini, Farini, Hera, and Carl Lentini. Also to be remembered, without doubt, is the above-mentioned Salerno, born Adolf Behrend, and Willy Rossio, who had created an act called Direkt vom Bahnhof (Straight from the Station), in which he entered the stage with a workman who passed him suitcases and other elegant travel accessories with which he started to juggle. Another noteworthy Italian name was Antonio Vivalli, made famous by the legendary P.T. Barnum, who engaged himself in memorable duels with jugglers claiming to be as able as he.

Selma Braatz, born 1885 in Berlin, was the first female juggler to demontrate feats that were ordinarily performed by men. Another top gentleman juggler was Felix Adanos, who lived in Vienna. During the 40 years of his artistic career, Adanos also worked in variety theatres and circuses.

Today, the last surviving exponents of the variety art form are only found in Germany, by the juggler Jeton. He spent a year at the school Ecole de Cirque de Bruxells and found in Germany an exceptional teacher in the person of Arthur Caral, who was himself a strongman and salon juggler.

1 In the sense that Umberto Eco attributed at the end of *Lector in Fabula*, Milano, Fabbri-Bompiani-Sonzogno-Etas, 1979, p. 239.

2 de Banville, Theodore, *Memoires et pantomimes des Fr res Hanlon Lees*, Paris, Chez tous le Libraries, 1879, p. 178.

3 Ibidem, p. 177.

4 Wickham, Glynne, *Storia del teatro*, Bologna, Il Mulino, 1988, p. 468.

5 Founded by B.F. Keith and directed by E.F. Albee, who assumed complete control in 1918, when Keith died.

6 Play of words where "rats" written backwards is "star."

7 Slide, Anthony, *The Encyclopedia of Vaudeville*, Westport, Connecticut and London, Greenwood Press, 1957, p. 69.

8 Ibidem, pp. 167-169.

9 Valentine, Maggie, *The Show Starts on the Sidewalk*, New Haven and London, Yale University Press, 1994, p. 77.

10 Cain, Georges, *Anciens Théatres de Paris*, Paris, 1906, p. 56.

11 Meldolesi, Claudio, Gli Sticotti, *Comici italiani nei teatri d'Europa del Settecento*, Rome, Italy, 1969, p. 16.

IV

MOVING WITH THE TIMES

JUGGLING, SLAPSTICK AND SILENT MOVIES

The constant demand for new acts for the always-growing circuses and variety theatres started up a phenomenon of mixing within the genres. Among the new disciplines was the "comedy juggler." One of the first exponents of this new genus was Paul Petras, who in 1890 performed with his wife and son. The three appeared dressed as Pierrot. Named the Petras Trio they are cited here, above all, for being the first jugglers to give, even if only a small contribution, to the fine net of exchanges on the various levels between the variety and the silent movies. This ruined the repertoires of the variety, enriching firstly the players but being the principle cause for the end of the genre. Thanks to his particular skill, Paul Petras was chosen by the Marx Brothers and Emil Skladanowski to appear in the first film ever shown before a paying public. The projection was made with the Bioscope on November 1, 1895, in one of the major variety theatres of that era—the Wintergarten in Berlin.

The success of theatres such as the Wintergarten had, however, allowed many advances in the folk-performances. Also, to increase enjoyment, the habit of sitting in warm, comfortable and elegant surroundings was introduced to watch performances, which only a few years beforehand, the spectators would have been forced to watch crowded around a dusty crossroad—even on a rainy day. The public could watch the shows with fewer distractions and the comics weren't forced to attract their attention with crude cries and overly visible costumes but could start to build real scenes with more and more refined mechanisms.

Some of these mechanisms were then adopted by the American silent movies and called slapstick. In slapstick, every single ridiculous happening was the cause of the next, in a constantly increasing intensity, inevitably destined to provoke extremely loud laughter. The best example is the "cake in the face" gag, which may start with a bit of cream slipped by mistake onto someone's jacket, but ends with a hoard of people getting

CARL BAGGESEN

pies in their faces. The jugglers who intended to give their performance a mostly comical taste, however, had already included these components. One of the funniest jugglers to take on these techniques was the Danish performer, Carl Baggesen.

Baggesen was born in 1854 and in his youth he was a talented contortionist, known in the German variety as Klischnigg. While he toured the United States with his wife Sophie, a discreet juggler, he realized the increasing success of the eccentric and humoristic artists. He therefore decided to make the most out of his natural comic verve—creating an act and tempting fortune. The most fashionable jugglers in that epoch were, above all, those from the "restaurant," however, representing cleverness in these had the upper-hand over comedy.

With Baggesen, the opposite happened. The curtain opened on a hotel room where the waitress, his wife Sophie, juggled three apples. A moment later, Carl entered. He wore a hotel waiter's suit, which was too big for him, with a portion of the shirt hanging out at his vest. His wife, ignoring all of this, looked towards the audience with a glazed look. Sophie tried to attract his attention but he continued to ignore her. She then asked him if he would be so kind as to pass her the plates so that she could continue with her juggling. This started the troubles for poor Baggesen. He picked up a plate, which slipped from his hand and broke into a thousand pieces. In his attempt to avoid this, he dropped another. Then his hands stuck to some flypaper, which from that moment on became a powerful tool of destruction. Every time he skimmed a plate, it stuck to his hands and, moving his body, he smashed the plates against the table or something else. All this with a stupid facial expression, which was similar to that which, a few years later, would bring success to the comedian Buster Keaton.

In the end, he was able to stack a high pile of plates; but he tripped, thanks to the flexibility of his body from many years of contortion, and he was able to bend and fall in such a way that he didn't break anything. He stood up calmly, with a sigh of relief, and let all the plates crash to the floor. The act was well thought-out. Every movement had a reason, every plate was broken for a reason, and he wasn't just wildly throwing things on the floor. When finished, only one plate remained in his hands but with overwhelming joy even this dropped and Baggesen ended his number submersed in porcelain fragments with much applause and laughter from the audience. Carl Baggesen died in 1931 after retiring from his profession at the age of 81. It's been calculated that during his career, he probably broke around six million plates!

The broken plates routine remained a classic of the circus comedy. Chaplin replicated Baggesen's gag for his *The Circus* in 1928, with Erwin Buehl playing the comic. Nowadays, the clown David Larible, actual star of the Ringling Bros., and Barnum & Bailey Circus presents a revised and corrected version of that number with great success, in which the artist uses some of the audience as his assistants.

COMEDY JUGGLERS

The evolution of another famous comic juggler's career, the American W.C. Fields, is living witness to how the rapport between silent films and variety theatre was becoming closer and more complicated. William Claude Dukenfield was born in 1879. His father had a billiard hall and young William first learned to juggle with apples and then changed to using the balls from his father's tables. At the start of his career, he made a costume using his mother's old clothes and for this reason he had adopted the style of a vagabond. He was, however, a gentleman vagabond walking with a slouch. He used common objects as props, such as top hat, walking stick, cigar boxes and three balls he played with at the billiard table.

Once he reached certain ability, W.C. Fields was hired in large entertainment parks until he judged himself good enough to pass for the definitive road of vaudeville. The splendid welcome that he received in such surroundings was due to the fact that, in the meantime in the United States, there were types of comics who influenced prejudices of race and class. The blackface and the Jew were types of racial comics whereas the tramp was one of class. The latter was the one who had the most success perhaps because, in contrary to the others, he was able to inspire a certain tenderness, even for the pragmatic American public.

W.C. Fields

WALL PAINTING AT THE OLD BERLIN CAFE, WINTERGARTEN: KING REPP, ENRICO RASTELLI, REBLA, GASTON PALMER, PAOLO BEDINI, PILETTO, TRIXIE.

After having worked for a period abroad, particularly in Europe and South Africa, W.C. Fields obtained a princely 10-year contract with the famous Florenz Ziegfeld, the theatre man who became famous for his farce variety performances, the Ziegfeld Follies, which changed year after year, always with growing success at the box office. Ziegfeld booked the best talents around and had, for example, hired Will Rogers as well, who was proficient with a lasso. However, W.C. Fields and Will Rogers weren't hired for being masters of their disciplines but for the quality of their comedy. In the course of time, W.C. Fields had, in fact, left the juggling route and refined a rather personal comedy based on gags that were often filled with social-political satire tied in with factual arguments. Another innovation was made when W.C. Fields started to write and interpret short comic films, such as *Million Dollar Legs* and *My Little Chickadee*.

After he had given up juggling, W.C. Fields even gave up his tramp character so that he could dedicate himself to complicated roles, such as Humpty Dumpty in *Alice in Wonderland* and that of Micawber in *David Copperfield*. What, more than anything else, was remembered by his affectionate fan-base was his image of a friendly tramp who, on posters and post-cards, survived even after his death in 1946 from the excessive alcohol consumption that plagued him throughout his life. Other jugglers became famous comedians, such as Eddie Cantor, Fred Allen, Joe Cook and Jimmy Savo.

Another juggler who introduced unheard-of comedy routines with a special flavor into his act, without however letting himself be influenced by the language of the comic films of the time, was Albert James Stevens—known as Rebla. Rebla had learned the first secrets of the trade with a troupe of Agoust's restaurant jugglers. With his robust physique, he wore an evening jacket with a small bow tie that, instead of having it around the collar of his shirt, he wore directly on his neck, around his Adam's apple. Even though he was able to carry out complicated exercises, Rebla made everything seem extremely easy, giving the impression he was bored during his number, starting in this way a type of "phlegmatic juggler." He almost seemed condemned to be a juggler—a sort of juggling prisoner. When he finished performing with, let's say, his cigar boxes, without waiting for the applause, he threw them briskly behind the curtains as if to rid himself in the quickest way possible, explaining his reasons to the audience. It was this that sparked off the hilarity as the spectators felt in some way personally involved in the performance.

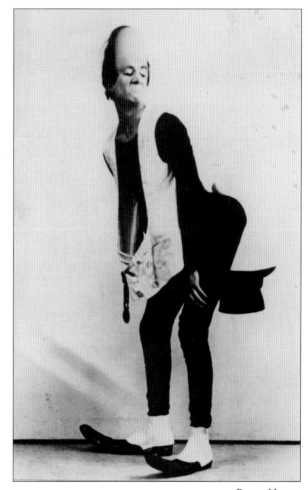

"The Laziest Juggler on Earth" was how the English performer Tom Elder Hearn was known. He was one of the first performers around 1910 to travel from job to job via airplane. Comedy juggler Rich Hayes was among the best practitioners of the variety-theatre artform. He played a cheerful Robinson Crusoe and performed extremely frugal-looking artistry with the aid of his black factotum, Friday. Australian Stan Kavanagh, neither gentleman nor tramp, instead looked like a leftover comic from a Mac Sennett movie. Bob Du Pont was called the "Prince of American Comedy Jugglers" when working in London in the late-1930's.

American juggler Lew Hoffman played an eccentric character dressed in a top hat and tails that accentuated his long arms. Ben Beri was yet another American juggler who combined

RICH HAYES

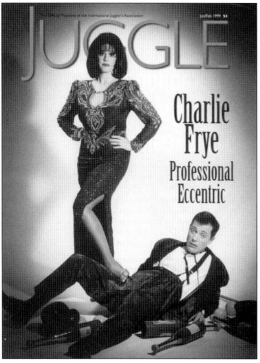

CHARLIE FRYE & CO.

DIETER TASSO

nonstop comedy with flawless club and ball work. The most famous juggling comedian in Germany was King Repp. He was the first performer to introduce custom-made top hats in a variety of colors, which were much better to see than ordinary black top hats at reflecting the stage lights. From a well-known Australian juggling family came Topper Martin. His parents, Victor and Maude Martin, as well as Topper's sister Decima, settled in England in 1920. Topper began working as a solo act in London when he was 17, performing as a juggler, magician, and sometimes as a banjo player.

A current member of the new generation of comic-eccentric jugglers is American Charlie Frye, born in 1961 in Virginia. He is a skilled physical comedian who succeeds in his juggling efforts despite a lack of cooperation from his assistant (and wife) Sherry. As mentioned elsewhere, Harrigan is acknowledged to have been the first juggler to talk on stage, around 1895; before him, jugglers were just assumed to be "dumb acts," the theatrical slang for non-speaking performers.

French artist Gaston Palmer was, in the 1930's the funniest of all talking jugglers. Twenty years later, mimicking moody people was the strength of the Australian juggler Rob Murray, who was a protégé of Rebla. Michael Davis is America's most eminent talking juggler of today. His act consists of very few jokes and not very much juggling technique. The mainstay of his performance is the timing and delivery, which is so slow and well-contructed that the audience is constantly hanging on every word. His hilarious signature trick is to juggle an egg, an apple, and a "razor-sharp" bowling ball. Berlin-born Dieter Tasso is a talking juggler from the old glory variety days. He became well known in 1952 when he performed his cup-and-saucer trick on a slack-wire for Ringling Bros., and Barnum & Bailey Circus in America.

Throughout the years, a number of solo jugglers worked in full partnership with each other. The comedy juggling in these duos varies as much as that of the individual artists discussed above—silent or talking, eccentric or straight, or often a combination of styles within a single act. Americans produced some outstanding examples of the eccentric-type of talking juggling teams, like the couple Waldo & Woodhead or the Flying Karamazov Brothers.

THE DISCOVERY OF LEISURE TIME AND WORK TOYS

At the end of the 1800's, with the definite advent of the industrial creation in the west, most city inhabitants started to feel the necessity to better occupy themselves in their leisure time. In general the games, and in particular the sports attracted increasing interest from the population, so much so that they reopened the new Olympic Games in 1896 in Athena. On its own account, juggling as a discipline, seemed to develop and was open to many innovations. The variety theatres were in a continuous search for original acts to entertain their public. The artists who wanted to emerge, or somehow have a constant influx of work, couldn't stop thinking for a moment of how to propose new unseen acts. The spectators had, furthermore, shown pleasure in finding everyday objects in the theatre.

The artists, sensitive to the public's wishes, adopted ways to introduce sporting and leisure accessories in their act. In this way, they were not only able to change their performances but to present situations and well-known objects so that the public could fully appreciate the difficulty of what they did—along with elegant costumes which, for the major part, represented those leisure activities

ROB MURRAY

ANITA BARTLING

HARRY LIND

THE FIVE NORMANS

that were, by then, a must. Part of the daily routine appeared to be wearing sporting clothes and hence, we see the the first "sports jugglers." In 1874, the American Bilton toured for the variety theatres with scenery that depicted an entire tennis court in which he juggled with rackets and balls. Another stimulating tennis juggler between 1928 and 1957 was the Frenchman Paul Berny. The tendency enveloped even female jugglers such as Anita Bartling, in the first two decades of the 20th century, who showed herself to be a good sports juggler.

The club—an accessory that today is considered belonging exclusively to jugglers—was a century ago considered to be a piece of sporting apparatus. Club swinging was a well-spread gymnastic activity in that there were official competitions up until 1932 and that, as often happens in these cases, was often used as a pastime and as a sport. It seems that the club was derived from an Indian instrument of war, the gada. After the English colonization of India, a part of the British forces understood the benefits to health of swinging the gada and adopted such exercises in their training. This pastime, consequently, spread also to the United Kingdom. However, in 1880, it took an American clown to introduce this object in the circus ring for the first time, using it in his clown act.

The club seems to have been built especially to be juggled and was quickly used in this discipline until it became a principal prop. The first juggler to use it in his act was the American, Rawson. The Australian Morris Cronin largely contributed to its widespread use when, around 1900, he too imported it into Europe. Cronin performed with his troupe of five people using metal-covered clubs, which the troupe members passed under their arms, legs, and behind their backs that shone under the electric lights. The artists that used these props were so numerous that soon factories producing handmade clubs were born, among that of a factory owned by the American

Edward van Wyck, founded in 1895, and thereby winning a place in history. When Harry Lind, from Jamestown, New York, retired as a juggler in 1919, he opened a manufacturing shop for clubs.

THE DEVELOPMENT OF CLUB-PASSING TROUPES

The Americans Alburtus & Bartram were around 1900 the first club-juggling act by two people to create a big name for themselves and start a demand for double-club jugglers. Derendo & Breen were the first act to throw fast shoulder throws with clubs. Ben Mowatt was, in 1895, the first man to figure out tricks for a three- and four-person act. Well-known American club-passing troupes around 1900 were the Normans, McBanns, the Kenyon Brothers, and Mike Fitzgerald and his Eight-Club Juggling Girls. Americans brought club-juggling to Europe at around the turn of the 20th century. One of the first American juggling troupes to appear in Europe was Morris Cronin's five-person team.

THE WALLASTONS

One of the most famous troupes to engage in this discipline was the Wallastons, founded by the Marquis Wilhelm von Seyffertitz. Born in Vienna in 1887, von Seyffertitz ran away from home at 18 to join a small traveling circus, where he learned to juggle. He formed a troupe of six that he decided would be called Wallastons, a name with an American flavor. In 1909, the Wallastons debuted at the Walhalla Theatre in Berlin and for two decades constructed a firm reference point for those who intended to specialize in club juggling. However, the Marquis Wilhelm von Seyffertitz had numerous disagreements with various exponents of the national socialist party and, when they came to power in 1933, he was forced into a decade of inactivity. The 6 Ferdini's, founded in 1920 by Kurt Kathert-Elsys, performed the largest German act including boomerang hats and club juggling. The most outstanding American hat-juggling troupe was the Elgins, who teamed up in the mid-1930's.

3 *ELSYS*

The troupes of club jugglers had such success, and became so widespread, that it quickly became a performing standard for almost every circus or variety theatre. The make-up of these acts was all very similar. We can, therefore, dwell upon a description of the Mongador's club routine. In this way, we get an idea how, from the 1920's up until today, one routine has been seen by millions of people, whether with some small or large changes. There has been a common format in countless troupes from then until now.[1] The elegance, harmony and originality with which they performed make them without doubt very worthy representatives of this category.

George, Ninette and Anne Mongador together with another partner (changed more than once in the course of their careers), were the first artists who had their own stage backdrop. It was a simple but elegant dark blue curtain with their name in big letters that sparkled under stage nights. Their moderate costumes were very sophisticated and their white clubs had an uncharacteristic form with a rounded end that made them seem like small baseball bats. The formation that was ideal was that of two women, a man and a comic. They started their act with everyone doing different tricks. While a woman juggled three diamond-studded torches, another juggled bouquets of flowers. The third juggled a hat, gloves and a cane. The comic was appropriately dressed, making balls appear and disappear from his waistcoat. In this way, they were able to show from the start their different abilities.

When the two started to pass the clubs between them,

THE ELGINS

the sidetracked comic—reading a newspaper and smoking a cigar—ended up finding himself in the "firing line" and losing his newspaper and cigar, which were hit by the clubs. The successive exercise consisted in passing the clubs in "three's," with one in the middle making the "bridge"—a not-so-easy arrangement due to the different positions of throwers and catchers. Even more difficult was passing 12 clubs between four people requiring accurate precision. One of the liveliest figures was the "leap frog" in which an artist came behind the shoulders of another, who was juggling three clubs, and leapt over and stole the clubs and carried on juggling. A variation of this was the "shove," which consisted of pushing a juggler away from under his pattern, substituting him, without changing the rhythm of the exercise.

The Mongadors are also credited with the creation of the "moving juggler," in which the juggler is lifted up but continues to juggle even in a horizontal position. Another of George Mongador's inventions (he had the comic part)

MONGADORS

was that of the "crazy juggler," who, after throwing the clubs haphazardly left and right, would bring them slowly back under his control. It is unnecessary to say that an exercise is only possible for one who already has technical mastery. To end their club routine, the Mongadors had two possible finales, the "fancy" and the "funny." During the former finale, three artists threw their clubs at the fourth member, who had to catch them and then re-throw them out again, all the time changing the angles at which he threw them. The second version was none other than a comic variation of the first, in which he who received the clubs, instead of throwing them again, kept them and held them in his hands, putting one between his legs, another under his arms and so on, until he ran out of space.

The Mongadors also used more original props, such as rings and plates, the latter more difficult to handle due to their smooth and slippery form. The combinations with the plates ended in two variations similar to those of the clubs, the "petite" and the "grand filade." The three artists threw their plates at the comic, who to hold them had to keep them in "petite filade"—in other words, put them in two rows on a table with a table cloth "grand filade." Some throws were deliberately off-course to force the comedian to make

BREMLOVS

exhilaratingly acrobatic catches. In the grand filade, furthermore, when the two piles were perfectly ordered, the comic gave a sign of satisfaction and then tripped over the table-cloth breaking all the plates on the floor.

The Carlton Sisters were a group of five Englishwomen who excelled in the use of elegant and evocative costumes. Female troupes became somewhat more common over time in the mid-1930's. The R. Tanne Company, from Germany, consisted of four young women and one man who juggled with glittering clubs. The four Italian sisters known as Sorelle Rolandi, were floor acrobats as well as lightning-speed club-passers. Family traditions have been especially important to Italian, Spanish, and Czech performers, as can be seen in the history of the Spanish club-passing troupe D' Angoly's, the descendants of the famous Briatore Family of performers. In 1958, the Briatore Family split up, with the members starting new groups (Alegria Brothers and Biarges), mainly with their own children. After World War II, the Czechoslovakian troupe 5 Bremlovs set new standards for club-passing. In 1954, the Budapest-based Circus School brought out the 5 Villams, who combined acrobatics with fast club-passing. Plates, rings and boomerangs whizzed through the circus ring when the Three Munteanus, from Romania, appeared.

Fredy Berousek, from the Czech Republic, descends from a sixth-generation Czech circus family. He performed as a catcher in a flying trapeze act and formed in the mid-'80s—with his wife Sonja and two sons Mario and Robert—the club-passing troupe 4 Fredis.

Many American club-passing ensembles emerged in the mid-1970's and included the Flying Karamazov Brothers, Amazing Fantasy Jugglers, Bay City Reds, Passing Fancy, and Airjazz, a three-person team of Kezia Tenebaum, Peter Davison and Jon Held. The group, which has kept Boulder, Colorado as its home base since 1982, has earned an international reputation. By the 1980's, most of the large juggling troupes (more than three performers) had disappeared. The financial costs of performing in a large group prohibited professional-quality acts from touring. Most of the juggling acts in the 1980's and 1990's were duos. Well known in the United States became the Gizmo Guys (Barrett Felker and Allan Jacobs), the Raspyni Brothers (Dan Holzman and Barry Friedman), the Passing Zone (Owen Morse and Jon Wee), and Doubble Troubble (the twins Alex and Nick Karvounis). They all set a high standard for team club-passing mixed with comedy and talking.

RASPYNI BROTHERS

SPORTING PROPS

Jugglers didn't limit themselves to sporting props, and they passed rapidly onto using leisure items. One of the most popular pastimes of that time was billiards. Elegant, or less formal, the billiard rooms were to be found in every small town and were always busy. Often, it was the

DOUBBLE TROUBBLE

same people crowding the billiard halls during the day who went to watch the variety shows in the evening. They found it surprising, therefore, to see one of their favorite accessories on stage—the table with the green cloth. The first juggler to have the idea of taking a billiard table on stage was A.W. Asra. His real name was Waldemar Paetzold and he was born in Berlin in 1873. Other than juggling with billiard balls and cues, which had already been done before by others, he had based his act on a proper billiard game played against himself, in search of even more different performances.[2] The balls that he struck with great mastery bounced everywhere, creating spectacular figures, and they even bounced out of their correct place to land on his head. He thereafter increased the visual effect of the show having his wife, Greta, hold various targets of differing sizes and distances from the table, all of which the balls would hit.

Another representative of this strange but appreciated discipline was Feliciano Trewey, born in 1847, who ran away from his wealthy family to join a small circus that had taken him on as a helper. Around 1910, after starting to juggle with potatoes, he decided to turn his passion for billiards into a routine that he performed in black tights wearing a white hat. He was never tired of his cues and the show often went on even after the perform-ances, engaged into the early hours with his friends and colleagues in infi-nite challenges that made his admirers go wild. Other similar acts were by the Berno's Duet and The Two Yvorys. Yvory's female partner, who Rudolf called "Princess of the Billiard Cannon," would fire a cannon at him while he rode around the stage on his unicycle grabbing the heavy balls that came from every direction. The female half of the Berno's swung on a low trapeze catching the balls that her partner shot off the table.

The fantasy of the jugglers seemed limitless and that concept of spare time was explored in every aspect. There was even a "juggling tourist," named Morie, who simulated a bicycle trip during which, finding himself with a puncture, started to take his means of travel to pieces and to juggle with the various bits. Thereafter, the bicycle

VILLAMS

started to take hold and cycle-jugglers appeared—grandchildren of the horseback jugglers. In fact, when the acrobatic cyclists, those mainly on a unicycle, thought about how to make their performances more impressive (and given that the only part of their body that was free was their hands), they started to insert elements of juggling in their routines.

Among these, Charlie Wood held his unicycle on a narrow raised platform. The Hungarian Chinko, who at the start of the last century was the first to juggle with 10 balls (throwing however two balls at a time), closed his performance with an original exercise—he took apart the various pieces of a Gramophone and juggled with the various bits while, from the acoustic horn, one could hear a voice crying for help. Other leisure objects used by some jugglers (among them Richieri from 1862 and Alexandrini from 1865) were puppets similar to Wibly-Wobblies or Weebles. The king of this genus was Guillaume Clement who, in 1923, performed at the Medrano in Paris using differently sized and weighted toys.

Another particular object that appeared in those days was the diabolo, coming from China, where it was called a Kouen-Gen and was considered a toy. The diabolo is made up of two cones whose pointed ends are attached together to form a sort of dumbbell shape. This then sits on a string that has two sticks attached to its ends. The diabolo is based on the same principle of that of the yo-yo, the string giving it its fast spinning movement. The difference between the diabolo and its more famous cousin, the yo-yo, is that the diabolo can be thrown and caught on its string.

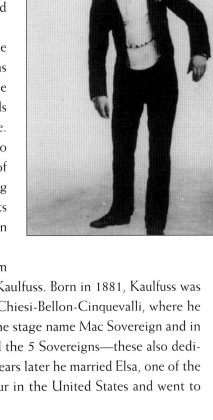

CHINKO

The first juggler to have the good idea to transform this toy into a juggler's prop was the Berliner Arthur Kaulfuss. Born in 1881, Kaulfuss was hired at an early age to work with the noted troupe, Chiesi-Bellon-Cinquevalli, where he worked in aerial acrobatics.[3] Afterwards he adopted the stage name Mac Sovereign and in 1903 he left the group to make one of his own, called the 5 Sovereigns—these also dedicated themselves to acrobatics at great heights. Two years later he married Elsa, one of the artists in the troupe. In 1907 he found himself on tour in the United States and went to

MAC SOVEREIGNS

see some friends who performed at the colossal Barnum and Bailey Circus.

The circus is now as it was then, a type of microcosm—a society inside a society whose customs, behavior and even simple pastimes spread with great rapidity. The preferred pastime of the circus artists at that time was the diabolo, which had been introduced by a troupe of Chinese artists. It was the first time that Kaulfuss had seen such a strange object and understood straight away its spectacular potential. He realized its versatility and that same year debuted with a new routine. Then it was normal practice in the larger troupes to be able to present at least a couple of routines to be able to get a reasonable wage. Kaulfuss continued to perform with the 5 Sovereigns but also presented a second routine with the diabolo that he continued to improve. One afternoon, while he was training in the theatre where he would be performing that evening, he threw the diabolo much too high by mistake and it got caught up with the electric cables suspended in the air. The object rolled down the whole length of the cable to end up next to the wall. This episode helped him realize how he could make his performance even more impressive by attaching cables in the hall.

Kaulfuss, therefore, put himself to work to devise a series of props made up of long cables, allowing him to send the diabolos along long and complicated routes above the audience. Among the registered objects there was the "diabolo tennis," a fine rope net against which he had his diabolo bounce, and the "windmill," a device that allowed the diabolo to also move vertically. In 1927, Kaulfuss, by then known by his stage name—Mac Sovereign—left aerial acrobatics to completely dedicate himself to his invention. In 1947, after he had attained much success throughout the world, Mac Sovereign decided to retire.

THE COLORED LEGION

In the first half of the 1800's, the jugglers and acrobats were still called mountebanks and were forced to perform in the squares and markets where they often didn't earn enough on a daily basis. Their category had undergone a profound transformation in a 20-year span. Suddenly, following the affirmation of the variety theatres and the smaller halls that could be found in every town, they had obtained an envious social status. Traveling around the world, no longer in broken-down carriages but using normal modes of transport and lodging in comfortable hotels, they earned more than respectable scholars or professionals; and were in contact with important people—writers, poets, painters, and actors.

Thanks to their frequent travels, to their agents and managers, and to the increasing spread of specialized magazines, they always knew what a hundred or so of their colleagues all over the world were up to, due to a sort of tom-tom effect helped by the growing development in the means of communication. If an artist inserted a new component in his act in New York, within a few days that same component was adopted, if not improved, by artists working in Vienna or elsewhere. The synchronization of all these factors was how the origin of the arrangement of the genres came about. Every step forward was spread, absorbed and surpassed in a relatively short period of time.

For about a century, from the second half of the 1800's up until a little before the start of World War II, the history of juggling wasn't only written by a few big names but also by a legion of artists, often thereafter forgotten. These artists were on a daily search to better their own performances, increasing the technical level and juggling with new objects, changing their style, the ambiance, the music, the costumes, the background for the act, and mixing the juggling with other acrobatic disciplines.

THE TECHNIQUE

The former group belong above all to the artists who went after the records, as was the case with Pierre Amoros, from the Werner-Amoros troupe, who was able to juggle nine balls. Then, and a few years later, he was an absolute first, surpassed eventually by the female juggler, Jenny Jaeger, who juggled 10 balls and in 1922 by Frank Le Dent, who juggled 11.

Jenny Jaeger, born in Odessa in 1910, started her routine juggling with balls and rings, and ended it using objects of a notable weight. Many of her pieces were new and some never to be equaled. Jaeger also performed at the last show held at the Wintergarten on June 20, 1944, before it was bombed by Allied aircraft. Still belonging to the first group, we find all those artists who had introduced new techniques, such as L.A. Street, who in 1898, started upside-down or reverse juggling. Instead of throwing the balls in the air, he threw them against the floor to catch them again after they bounced up. He was able to carry this

JENNY JAEGER

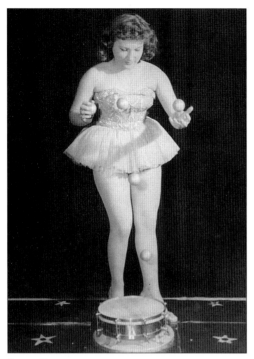

LULY PEREZOFF

WILLY WOLTARD

out with up to eight balls. Anita Bartling, in 1910, was able to play a big drum with seven balls, quickly surpassed by Kaethe Gueltini, who started to perform in 1908 and by 1920 was able to juggle with eight balls on a drum. Luly Perezoff, from the Omonima Family, was also able to perform this same feat.

One act that was invented in France in those years, was that of *les chapeaux volants* or *les chapeaux dansants*, in which cone-shaped hats flew about the stage from one head to another, without ever touching the ground. In the end, the hats were all collected in a tall pile by one of the group's members. The same act was also carried out by the Seroggs Trio, in 1888, at the Hagenbeck Circus and, thereafter, by the Americans Moran & Wiser, Fred Hardy and by Kurt Kathert (Ferdini) from Germany. Willy Woltard kept his audiences in stitches with a routine called The Terrible Millinery Shop. His stage set was a hat salon with all kinds of different hats.

The members of Chas Francois troupe had adopted costumes and make-up that gave them a devilish aspect. Other artists, on the other hand, used soft hats that seemed impossible to balance. These were, however, struck with long thin sticks that made them spin and stay still as if suspended in mid-air. Among these were Palermo and Phillips, plus the Peiros from South America.

Other props that were juggled, to the amazement of the audience, were banjos. In 1920, Franco Piper played and juggled with them at the same time. In 1900, the Goldeno Trio carried out a routine with spinning tambourines that took the place of the 32 spinning plates of their previous invention involving Indian scenes also demonstrated by the French trio Arizona's, a group that juggled with axes and other objects.

Gaston Palmer, who became famous as the "talkative juggler," was also successful with his routine with eight teaspoons that, in one gesture, all ended up in eight glasses all on the same tray. Straight away this exercise had numerous followers, like for example the Swiss juggler, Charles Carrer, who put 10 ice cubes, 10 lemon slices and 10 cherries onto a tray and in three moves made them fly into 10 glasses. With the same system, Ferry Mader, born in 1855, put 10 knives in 10 apples, and 12 candles in a candelabra with 12 arms.

There are two forms of equilibrium, one active and the other passive. The first is when the artist balances himself on an unstable object. The latter (passive) is one in which the artist makes use of his own body to balance inanimate objects. The German Hans Arrino, in 1890, performed in a strongman act in which he balanced a mass of three chairs, a table, and five barrels. The latter had water pouring out of them which filled the barrels below them from which, in their own turn, filled the barrels below them and so on.

STYLE

O n the other hand, many artists changed their style, props, costumes, music and the settings for their acts. Here are the eccentric jugglers, beloved by Marinetti, who carried out their acts in a succession of little and large tricks that had noteworthy success.[4] The eccentrics were, above all, American and the most famous were the Johnson Brothers, Art and Ben Mowatt as the New York Brothers, and especially Bobby May.

Bobby May was born in 1907 in Cleveland, Ohio, and when he was barely an adolescent, he realized that in those times there were so many jugglers that to become famous it might be necessary to build a routine with a completely new structure. In 1925 he performed in a duet, called Joe Cody and Partner, that he left in 1930 to debut as a soloist at London's Palladium. May is attributed with the invention of numerous feats, such as that of the simultaneous lighting and tossing of a match and cigarette, or, even more spectacular and difficult, that of lighting a match held between his teeth struck on the floor carrying out an Arabic somersault, i.e., sideways. Another one of his creations was that of the clever balls which, after having been thrown in all directions, always returned to end up in his top hat. He died in 1981 in Euclid, Ohio.

SIX MOWATTS

BOBBY MAY

THE COMBINATION OF DISCIPLINES

There have been many combinations of juggling with other disciplines, such as acrobatics—two disciplines already very hard on their own. Around 1900, Joseph Wallenda, from the celebrated ropewalking family, performed his juggling balanced on a smooth sphere, which he rolled under his feet. Alma Clara Jordan, wife of the tightrope walker Ben "Melas" Abdullah, was known as the lady juggler on a globe. Like "The Frenchman," Johnson Lee, around 1900, who not only walked around the stage on a large sphere but performed difficult feats, such as juggling with two balls and four clubs or balancing a peacock's feather on his nose while he played the trumpet. Julian Barillo performed on a rola-bola, a type of wooden cylinder, which has a slab of wood acting as a platform for the juggler. At the end of the 1800's, Kiners climbed a pyramid of tables balancing a full jug on his head. He then held a chair between his teeth on which a woman comfortably sat.

ARIZONA'S TOMAHAWK JUGGLERS

The most spectacular combinations could be those of jugglers and balancing acrobats. At the start of the 1900's, the 4 Uessems, who performed in the German theatres, walked in a head-to-head balance on top of a large sphere, while juggling with balls and rings. Another famous troupe was that of the Van de Velde & Co. Elly Van de Velde was able to balance upside down on the neck of

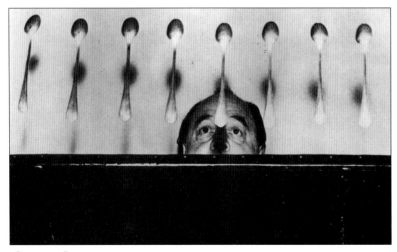

GASTON PALMER

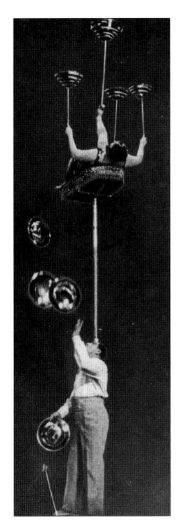

JOSEPH BLANK COMPANY

her brother while juggling with three balls. Their roles were then inverted and the brother balanced on Elly's head while juggling three balls and spinning a long pole with his feet, which had flags blowing at the ends. Elly was the also the first woman to balance on only one finger, which she put in a bottle.

The three Philipp brothers (Karl, Max, and Erich) were also talented juggling equilibrists. At the start of World War I, they split and the younger started up the Erich Philipp Company, in which his wife and a partner also worked, both of whom were able to perform sensational feats. In one of these, Erich put himself in the usual position for an antipodist, which is lying down belly up, with his legs in the air. He held a barrel on his feet, which contained his wife, and on his wife's head the partner balanced on one foot only. All three in the meantime juggled with four plates each, including Erich on his back. Also, the other brothers, Karl and Max, created a routine—the Four Philipps—which executed similar feats.

Another troupe of this genre was the Joseph Blank Company, a group that was no-less talented and which was comprised of leader Joseph, born in 1887, a multi-talented artist, and Mary, one of the strongest woman

KARL, MAX & ERICH PHILLIPP

jugglers of that time. Joseph juggled with four large metal plates while balancing a three-foot-long metallic tube on his forehead. At the top of the tube there was a sort of rigging, the antipodist's equipment, where his sister sat upside down and in every hand and foot, and even between her teeth, she held two canes on which plates spun.

The tradition of the horseback jugglers, born with the start of the circuses, went on until the 20th century. In 1910, the most important representatives in this category were a Russian and an Italian. The Russian, Nikolai Akimowitstch Nikitin, was the adopted son of the director of the Fratelli Nikitin Circus who, in the course of his career, changed his repertoire many times, therefore ending

PEARSON AND HANDY ANDY

LUCY GILLET

up with one very vast repertoire. The objects used for juggling were candelabras, with the appropriate candles, tennis rackets, fire torches and balls. He alternated the horseback routines with those on his own feet. The Italian, Vittorio Ferroni, of Russian origin, used roughly the same props as his rival, Nikitin, adding a folkloristic touch. Standing up on a horse, he juggled with a ball on his forehead, bouncing it in time with the music that he, himself, played with his mandolin, while carrying out the Awata Games with a ball that his partner threw to him from the center of the ring. Emile Aguinoff wore a sporting costume and juggled with seven balls and five knives. Pearson and Handy Andy were very elegantly dressed and juggled with hats, clubs, and beach balls while galloping bareback on a horse.

There were also many artists who introduced normal utensils into their acts. Adam Rudolf "Rapoli" Randerath, born in Aachen in 1848 (and married to Helena Schiffers in 1869), was first to have the idea of juggling while climbing the rungs of a ladder that wasn't resting upon anything, but, thanks to Rapoli's continual movements, the ladder remained in a vertical position. Such a routine is known as "equilibrium of a freestanding ladder." Rapoli's son, Rodo Leo, born in 1870, continued to improve on this new discipline, managing to juggle up to eight balls while on the freestanding ladder. Another artist to excel in this discipline was Leonardo Ferroni, son of the famous horseback juggler, who balanced on the ladder juggling up to six rings while holding a stick with a ball between his teeth, and another stick and ball on his forehead. Another good Italian artist was Ottavio Canestrelli, hired in the United States by the Ringling Bros.

In this group, the important and antique genre of antipodism returns—i.e., juggling with the feet while laying down, chest upwards, on a piece of equipment similar to a deck chair known as a trinca. This ancient discipline seems to have come from the east, even if traces have been found in South America, in the Court of Montezuma I. The artist, more than juggling, must often be able to bend his body in postures and have perfect coordination of his lower limbs. The western antipodists normally used the same objects as jugglers—balls, rings, plates and so on. However in 1871, Sylvester Schaeffer juggled with a table, a chair, a lamp and a large bed. Another good player in this discipline was Lucy Gillet, who started her act juggling with nine balls but who had specialized in antipodism and equilibrium. Other names were the Viennese master Mathias Machaz, or moreover Will Carr, who started his career after World War I and became a big name performing difficult feats. Another good talent was J. Ferroni, relative of the famous horseback juggler, who juggled with a barrel, a table and a giant bottle of champagne lying on an instrument precariously balanced on the end of a long pole. Jean Rudolph Amados, born in 1879, a great diabolo juggler, debuted in 1910 by performing upside-down, getting the diabolo going with his feet.

The animals that the audiences were able to see in those years, engaged in juggling activities, should be given a special mention. The Americans Robertus & Wilfredo, around 1900, had a fox terrier "assistant." The two jugglers Nova & Eveline possessed a crow, which took part in their act. Willi Nowack had tamed the crow, which had been found nearly dead, throwing it small pieces of food and substituting it slowly for clubs and balls. However, the star of these animal-jugglers was Bubu, a chimpanzee that had been tamed by the Danish juggler Viggo Benny. He performed a parody of Rastelli's act and, for this reason, was often included before or after the great juggler's routine to set the whole crowd laughing.

One of the finest novelty juggling acts in 1950 was Erik van Aro. This German artist played drums as he juggled the instruments themselves. The wildest number in the act of Dr. Hot and Neon (Bill Galvin and Steve Mock from the United States), was the juggling of six ukuleles, specially tuned, while plucking out an ethereal rendition of the Ode to Joy theme from Beethoven's Ninth Symphony.

WILL CARR

L.A. STREET

THE SCHAEFFERS: TRADITION AND INNOVATION

In most of the cases we have examined up until now, it has only rarely happened that a juggler has learned his technique in a paternal way, however, and when this happens we can see the formation of grand dynasties. One of the most symbolic cases of birth, affirmation, and disappearance of a true dynasty of artists is that of the Schaeffer family.

The founder of the dynasty, Karl Johann Schaeffer, was born in Prague in 1824 in a wealthy family. However, he was orphaned at just 15 years of age and made the decision of tempting fate by running away to follow a modest troupe of mountebanks. His life changed when he was accepted for an apprenticeship in the famous Karl Rappo group, who were then one of the most prestigious artists in Europe. In the Rappo group, Schaeffer was, above all, a partner in the specialty of the Icarian Games. However, after meeting such a master, he was able to build a vast basic repertoire in many acrobatic disciplines. Schaeffer had the ability to create, on the basis of the teachings that he had received, newer and ever-more spectacular feats, improving in a particular way his ability to juggle with his feet.

In 1857 he married Susanna Beisensteiner and had five children—Sylvester, Sidonie, Severus, Suzanne and Sebaldus. In those years every child was a potential member of the troupe. His main task became that of teaching his children what he, himself, had learned throughout his profession. Among his five children, all talented artists, the two males, Sylvester and Severus, emerged in a notable way. The father wanted both to excel in all stage disciplines, singing and dancing included, rather than particularly following juggling, antipodism and the Icarian Games.

In 1881, Sylvester was one of the first jugglers to change from the classical tasseled tights to an elegant evening suit, including top hat and gloves. In this way he started a new style destined to last until today and to be adopted by many jugglers. In France there are terms specifically indicating "he who comes from a circus family... *les enfants de la balle*," and "he who on the other hand came from outside... *les artistes de rencontre*." The motivation for jugglers who did not come from a circus family are, ironically, greater than those who were almost obliged to practice a certain discipline.

Being an exponent of a second generation of artists, as in Sylvester's case, is almost an ideal condition because, on one hand, he was accustomed at an

THE SCHAEFFERS

early age to the atmosphere and to rehearsals and, on the other hand, he wasn't set with the closed-mindedness of a suffocated tradition. Another detail that helped make Sylvester's fortune was that of always knowing how to adapt to the productive systems of the era. Sylvester quickly felt the need to create a small troupe that allowed him to offer, to managers and theatre directors, performances long enough to cover an entire show on their own. He looked for people already able, with good experience, when it came to putting together the troupes.

For example, he hired Julius Neumann (the ex-partner of Paul Conchas) for a while. Perhaps, because Sylvester was the most lacking in expertise among the others in his family, he distinguished himself as the inventor of new shows rather than as an artist. In 1899, he created an act destined to be unique in its genre, that of the Icarian on a horse. In this, some of the members of the troupe laid down on a horse. Using their legs as springs, they helped the more-agile members of the group carry out somersaults and other spectacular

SEVERUS SCHAFFER

figures. He delicately modified the combination of every aspect in their performances. For the Icarian horseback routine, for instance, he had costumes and music specially created in order to recreate and simulate a Spanish bullfight.

In an age when most of the artists were deprived of scenery, or had to use what was available in the theatres where they performed, Sylvester on the other hand made use of original scenery purposely made for his shows. He gained great success in the whole of Europe, visiting the major capital cities and even performing across the ocean at the famous Metropolitan Opera in New York. In 1902, he retired from the stage to devote teaching all the secrets of his art to his son, Sylvester Schaeffer II, who was also destined to have a successful career.

Severus, the second male child of father Karl Johann Schaeffer, wasn't any less able than his elder brother. He was soon aware of a propensity for acrobatics and chose to perfect his ability, becoming a solo virtuoso rather than work in a troupe. During the customary hard years of rehearsals and training, Severus closely followed the public's taste.

SYLVESTER JUNIOR

He made his stage entrance on a horse-drawn carriage. He wore an elegant riding coat and top hat, and by his side on the carriage seat, sat a beautiful, elegantly dressed child. After the carriage had left the scene, he quickly took off his elegant clothes to reveal a pair of smart black tights similar to that which the actors who played Hamlet might have worn. In this way, he started a series of extraordinary feats never seen before.

He was equally able to juggle with heavy objects as with extremely fragile ones. For example, he would throw a large jar, a large basin and a heavy bedside table. He would then start to juggle with six plates while balancing a cane on his forehead. Having put down his plates, he spun a wheel taken from the carriage on top of the cane. Still balancing horizontally on an arm above the jug, with the tip of his right foot he made the porcelain vase spin around, while behind his neck he held a candelabrum. With his free hand he spun six plates on the table's smooth surface.

Like his contemporary, Paul Cinquevalli, Severus alternated demonstrations of strength and beauty. He rolled a steel ball, which seemed to have a life of its own, along his back. Then, reaching his ankles, with a somersault, he made it return obediently between his hands. One of the feats that in 1892 had sent the Wintergarten's audience wild, was that of the "blind juggler"—that is to say he juggled blind-folded with an iron ball, a table, and a balled-up piece of paper! (A difficult enough feat, even with his eyes wide open, for the differing sizes of the objects used.) Following his great success he was hired in the major halls in Europe and also had the honor, across the ocean, to perform in front of an ex-president of the United States—Grover Cleveland. At the start of World War I, he retired to England where he died shortly thereafter.

Sylvester Junior, born in 1895, was known as one of the most diverse artists of that time and yet, as a child, he had such an emaciated physique that doctors had foreseen a future full of illnesses. Helped by his two sisters, Stella and Stefanie, who later on would become his assistants, Sylvester Junior strengthened and perfected his physique so much so as to be compared to a Greek athlete in adulthood. The Olympic Games inspired his act, in which he performed as a juggler, equilibrist, horse rider, bowman, dog trainer, and even painter, magician, violin wizard, and clown musician. It was his extraordinary versatility in each of these disciplines that earned him the title of the Universal Genius. This act was so long and intense that he was often given the entire second half of a variety show.

A few years before World War II, following some problems with several exponents of the national socialists, Sylvester Junior decided to transfer permanently to the United States, a land of which, he had never attempted to hide his fondness. In Hollywood, at the end of his career (as did many variety artists of that era), he used his copious talents in the making of some black-and-white films that, however, weren't very successful. He had a son, Peter, who dedicated himself entirely to music. When Sylvester Junior died in New York in 1949, the glorious dynasty of the Schaeffer family ended.

THE REVERHOS AND THE SPONTANEOUS CREATION

Among all these many multi-talented artists, who were able to mix in a unique act more than one discipline at the same high level, the three French Reverhos brothers without a doubt earn a place of honor. Madelein, Gustave and André were juggling ropewalkers and acrobats able to perform incredible exploits. What was, however, truly remarkable was that they had a spontaneous teaching. They weren't an actor's children and hadn't had any instructors nor anyone who might have taught the rudimentary techniques for the more difficult tricks. Their father was a master bricklayer and had two sons who had carried on this profession. To keep fit they went, however, to a gymnasium, an important place in those days of connecting sport and acrobatics. Remember that the founders of many Italian circuses—Bogino, Nicolodi, and Nones—had started to develop their acrobatic ability right in those gyms. Furthermore, it often happened that the artists found themselves on tour and not having places adapted to train in, so they headed to gyms to keep in training.

It was one of these artists, who by chance was training in the same gym that Gustave and André used, who had noticed their predisposition for acrobatics and suggested that they create their own act. In this way they started to train on their own, together with their sister. It could have been due to the natural

ANDRÉ REVERHOS

GUSTAVE REVERHOS

formation of their art, that they were able to blossom and fully express themselves without constrictions and conventions. They debuted in 1928 at the Empire, one of the most prestigious variety theatres in Paris. Dressed as Pierrot, the fascinating Madeleine, the athletic Gustave, and the friendly André, they started their act with the balls and sticks used in the Awata Games. After this, Gustave gracefully walked along a rope that, to increase the difficulty of the equilibrium, wasn't under tension. With harmonious movements he balanced on one hand on the rope, while he held a small stick between his teeth, on which he spun a plate, on his feet he turned an umbrella, that was opened inside out, and with his free hand he turned another opened umbrella. Ending this feat, close by, was his brother who head-balanced on a sphere, spun a ring on one leg while juggling three clubs. Then Gustave again, with one foot on the rope, turned a pole with his left hand with two little flags, while juggling three plates in his right hand, and between his teeth was a stick on which a ball was placed which was magically balanced on another stick and another ball.

Their attraction was a fusion of that of Rastelli and that of the Australian Con Colleano, another great figure in the international variety—the first man able to complete a forward somersault on a tight rope and perform crazy Spanish dancing.[5] The Reverhos had brought back one of the oldest and most popular juggling forms from the fairs, that which is performed on the ropes, taking them from the squares and markets into the elegant variety theatres of that epoch.

---

1   Adrian, *A vous les jongleurs* (art, figures, and personalities), Paris, Adrian, 1977, pp. 57-66.

2   Like the great Paul Cinquevalli also known as "The Human Pool Table."

3   Where he developed along with Paul Cinquevalli.

4   Marinetti, *Límmaginazione senza fili e le parole in libertà* in Verdone, Mario, Il Futurismo, Roma, Newton Compton, 1994, p. 30.

5   St. Leon, Mark, *The Wizard of the Wire*, Sydney, Aboriginal Studies Press, 1993, p. 220.

V

THE MYTH AND THE EMULATION

ENRICO RASTELLI... "THE" JUGGLER

Considered by many to be the greatest juggler of all time, Enrico Rastelli, born in 1896, died in 1931 being barely 34 years old. The first generation of Rastellis to enter into the show business world was Enrico's father Alberto and uncle Alfredo. They specialized in acrobatic juggling on a long pole, in antipodism, and in various aerial disciplines. They had left traces of their engagements in the variety theatres' programs from the end of the 1800's. In 1895, Alberto left his brother, who continued to perform solo, and married Giulia Bedini, who lived and had relations in Bergamo. She gave birth to an only child, Enrico, on December 18, 1986 during a stop of the Fedasewsky's Circus on the Volga in Russia.

The child passed part of his childhood on tour with his parents and part with his uncles in Italy. His parents, meanwhile, performed juggling and other acts in various circuses and variety theatres. An anecdote, much loved by circus historians, tells of how the young Rastelli was forbidden to practice the art of juggling, as it wasn't considered a lucrative activity. Enrico however, drawn by an untamable passion, practiced out of his parents' sight. It's easy to believe that the opposite was true, as Enrico himself recounts:

"It is certain that in the cradle I wasn't able to balance my bed on my nose, nor in my first attempts to walk did I pull off the table cloth in an attempt to juggle with the plates and cups without breaking them into a thousand pieces. Even I had to learn all

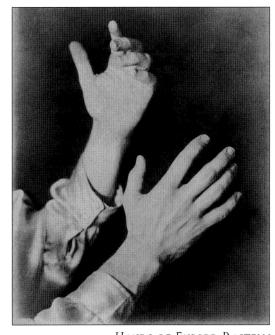

HANDS OF ENRICO RASTELLI

of this. When I was five, my father gave me five small balls. He said: 'Here you are my boy, do the best you can!' and I started to do what I could."[1]

In another interview, Rastelli tells of an experience that happened to him in his childhood:

"For my light weight and grace, I was an ideal subject to be thrown from the dome and it was a truly sensational sight to see a small girl thrown up in the air. So they had me working with a girl's wig on my head. This all went well until, at great public amusement, my wig fell off. This was a great blow to my pride and was the last day that I worked as an acrobat."[2]

In effect, in the circuses every parent tried to teach children the greatest number of disciplines possible until the family could perform three or four routines and, therefore, receive higher rewards. Let's remember that the younger members were more involved in putting up and taking down the big top, carrying the equipment, cleaning the horses and driving the wagons in the long hauls from one city to the next, even in cold and unfavorable weather. The Rastellis, who weren't swimming in money, did the same with Enrico, who had to learn a bit of it all at the start of his career. Therefore there were long, neverending rehearsals and training. Furthermore, to explain the elegance and grace that his admirers so often recognized in him, we can quote the dance lessons that he took in his youth from one of the major exponents of ballet in the 1900's—Vaslav Nijinskij.

In those years, the artists in the Russian circuses were obligated to learn how to move because a major portion of the shows were pantomimes, based on historical reconstructions, in which artists were compelled to take part. For almost all of his adolescence, Enrico took part in his family's acts and the pantomimes in the circuses, where they were hired, but

he, however, continued to train. When his parents, Alberto and Giulia, began to grasp the potential of their son, and after they realized that they had a true talent in the family, he could then finally start his career as a juggler. However in 1909, Enrico was still too young and the Talon Law, created in 1873 in France, forbade children under 15 years to perform alone.[3] They, therefore, built a show around him with a new act that included his parents—the Rastelli Trio.

In the making of their act, the Rastellis took into account the tendencies of that era, giving their performance an elegant impression without omitting to perform exceptional feats, such as that in which Enrico balanced his head on his father's, while both juggled four balls, three canes, or otherwise three or four burning torches.

RASTELLI FAMILY, ENRICO IN CENTER

The Rastelli Trio was an unusual routine of "Juggling, Equilibrists, Antipodists Head-to-Head." This type of the performance didn't represent an absolute novelty, but the response they obtained from audiences was enormous.[4] They naturally started to be asked for by the top managers of that time.

In 1915, Enrico debuted as a solo artist at the Truzzi Circus. He was 19 and his ability was by then well known. A little while later, on tour in Russia, Enrico met one of the best Asian jugglers ever to appear in the west—Takashima, the Japanese master of the so-called Awata Games. His act consisted of holding a stick between his teeth, on which one or more balls of differing sizes bounced and created endless figures. Blown away by the magnificence of these combinations, Enrico dedicated himself almost exclusively to the point where the ancient juggling styles met

ENRICO RASTELLI WITH HIS FATHER. AT RIGHT IS HIS ASSISTANT, UMBERTO SCHICHTHOLZ.

the style of the western artists of that time. When Rastelli saw Takashima make his beautiful stage entrance in his kimono, almost celebrating his act rather than performing it, Rastelli didn't "discover" but "understood" his profoundness. He understood how to pay homage to his work, making it solemn.

In 1912, when they returned to St. Petersburg after a tour in Sicily, the Rastellis remained in the destroyed territory where the Romanov's reigned. They would have probably remained there for good if, in 1919, father Alberto hadn't made the important and difficult decision to leave Russia, which was still shaken by the recent revolution. Finally in 1919, when they arrived in their homeland, after almost a decade of success on Russian soil, Enrico was almost unheard of. In 1921, the English agent Henry Sherek discovered him at the Manetti Circus while it was at Naples and he immediately offered him a contract to work firstly at the Alhambra, in Paris, where he was described as Le Plus Fameux Jongleur.[5] He was then hired to perform in an English variety theatre's circuit at 500 pounds a month.[6] In this way, he concluded, with relative ease, an important move towards the variety theatres to which he finally devoted himself.

The variety show in the 1920's was an ensemble of songs, dances, comic sketches, and circus acts that were considered by many theorists as a close relative of the circus.[7] However, for an artist, the difference between the two genres was abysmal. By working in variety or permanent circuses, one performed in elegant buildings, sojourned to comfortable hotels, moved from one place to the next in trains or by boat. On the other hand, working in a traveling circus, one performed under big tops, at times in poor conditions, living in carriages more or less welcoming, performing in the cold and putting up with long hauls. The virtuoso soloists had more possibility of working in variety theatres than in the circuses, where in the later they preferred to prepare colossal pantomimes or spectacular horseback performances (Horseplays?!), where the solo acts had very little space.

The closing down of the numerous animal cages, with the consequent transfer of the animals to the circus, had started up a change from equestrian shows to animal shows, in which the main part was made up of animal tamers.[8] Furthermore, it was the period between the two great wars when the variety had its unique period with a commercial system like that of the cinema today—with a sector dedicated to the production, one for the distribution, and one for the management, of the halls. The circus, conversely, wasn't able to keep up with the pace of the industrial life and the prefabricated shows.

With his entrance in the variety theatres, Rastelli found himself next to artists such as Loie Fuller, Fregoli, Petrolini, and Vittorio Podrecca and his Dwarf Theatre, and even Sarah Bernhardt, giving him a persona that created his myth and legend. The tour that went on until 1924 represented Rastelli's first engagement in a circuit, with the consequent possibility to come into contact with, and be confronted by, numerous artists who worked

TRIO RASTELLI

there. Life in the provincial English variety wasn't the best, for there were heavy fines for those who were found in a state of intoxication. Often the cast was only partly made up of good professionals, the rest were beginners who were not always destined for a rosy future. In order to avoid clashes between the artists, the director of the circuit reserved the right to choose the place and size of the names on the billboard.

In February of 1923, the Variety Artists' Federation Association, with around 1,000 members and having enormous power, published *The Era*—the official voice of its members—summarizing the dramatic annual conference. It explained how, in the less industrialized areas (in other words, where Rastelli performed), that the demand for artists had fallen in such a sharp way that it was even difficult for good acts to find a reasonable sequence of engagements. In fact, in Great Britain in the years immediately after World War I, an embargo was placed on all artists from enemy countries working in this sector.[9] Therefore, in all contracts a clause appeared underlining that neither the artist, nor anyone who took part in his act, could be German, Austrian, Hungarian, Bulgarian or Turkish. Italy was the country greatly gifted with a "close exoticism."

As well as playing the English circuit, Rastelli also helped open the doors of London's prestigious Olympic Hall. From December 22 until January 27, Rastelli performed at Bertram Mills' The Great International Circus.[10] Mills was one of the first circus directors to understand the importance of a good press office, and good public relations, and was able to attract the attention of the whole of London—the Royal Family included—who hurried to his shows and provoked an uproar in newspapers. The attention that the Royals gave to the entertainment form was already shown by the Royal Command Variety Performances, representations of variety put together especially for the Royal Family, once a year, starting in 1912.[11]

The *Stage Yearbook* of 1924 shows one of the worst years ever for the variety business, holding the new management systems responsible for the crisis—ahead of the up-and-coming plays and

RASTELLI IN KIMONO

musicals—under which the choice of the artists didn't depend on the local management anymore but by the superiors of the circuit, who staged a complete program. The *Stage Yearbook* added, however, that they could still save the capital's great theatres, which presented traditional shows. England was, furthermore, considered as a place of antique traditions—even the birthplace of variety—given that in London, in 1852, Charles Morton had opened history's first Music Hall.

Therefore, if the circuits of the urban suburbs were gray and difficult to put up with, the capital was still prestigious and lavish. It was here that Rastelli preferred to find his engagements. On the occasion of a performance at The Palladium, *The Era* wrote: "The show has been reinforced on Monday and comprises of 15 acts. There is also the novelty of the juggler, Enrico Rastelli, who demonstrates skill and fantasy in a quantity of feats never seen before."[12] A few days later: "Enrico Rastelli is a slender young man with a disarming smile who, however, knows how to juggle. His feats have the merit, above all, of being original and to turn the natural order of things upside down, in as much as many of them are carried out while he balances on his head. It doesn't often happen that a juggler

RASTELLI POSTER 1921

is put in the program as the star, but this skilled Italian has proved worthy."[13] Thanks to a memorandum in the archive of the British Music Hall Society, we discover that during his stay at the Coliseum, Rastelli was able to juggle 10 balls at once, an absolute first, which is difficult to beat even today.[14]

A year on tour in Europe gave Rastelli the chance to assess himself, with respect to the other artists on the market, and to help him recognize his own value. On December 14, 1922, Rastelli reached an agreement with one of the most-noted American agents, Herbert Marinelli, sealing a contract for an American tour with the Keith-Albee circuit, accepting a salary of $700 a week, and having his name well positioned on the billboard straight from the beginning.

His American debut happened in March 1923 at Keith's Theater in Boston. On March 12, the greatest name responsible for the most important American variety circuit in those years—Edward Albee in person—headed for the small theatre in Providence, in whose program Rastelli also appeared, to check the standard of the performances. At the end of the show, Albee sent a letter to the manager of the company, in which were listed his opinions of the acts and the eventual changes to be carried out. In recommendation of the juggler Enrico Rastelli, he wrote: "This man is a true revelation. Some of his features are surprising and some are seemingly impossible. An absolute triumph!"[15]

Rastelli was taken off the provincial circuit and put in the most important variety theatre in America—the Palace, in New York City. This theatre was the flagship of the Keith-Albee circuit. The elegant architecture wasn't to keep away the rich classes, nor intimidate the less well-off classes with an exaggerated luxury.[16] Also, for the position that it occupied in the center of Manhattan, the Palace had become the most prestigious of all the American variety theatres, such that the measure of a successful artist was to play the Palace, to perform at the Palace. Reporters and critics who went there, and described the quality of the performances in the pages of the most-read newspapers, also highlighted the high respect reserved for the Palace. It was right in that entertainment temple that Enrico Rastelli had one of his most significant successes, and the most interesting newspaper coverage.

The first version of his routine was meticulous and complete, eighth of 13 acts, and all the reviews were agreeable and genteel. Mark Henry in two parts wrote one review for the American publication *Billboard* in April of 1923. A detailed description of a performance of the juggler that would leave us perplexed these days but it was normal in those days—the occupation of a variety theatre critic was already an established profession for nearly half a century and *Billboard* and *Variety* were highly popular magazines.

"Enrico Rastelli. Seen Monday afternoon, April 9, Palace Theater, New York, genre: juggling, staging: divided in three parts, duration; 16 minutes. Rastelli is a "de luxe" juggler who presents his entire act with unusual skill and manipulating ability in an admirable way. After his stage entrance wearing a red velvet kimono decorated with a shade of coral, accompanied by an assistant elegantly dressed with white gloves and a beautiful girl with a flame-yellow dress decorated in black, the young Rastelli carries out feat after feat with a supernatural technique and style of a classy showman. He bounces a ball on his head and at the same time juggles with six plates, he spins a cane horizontally striking it with another that he holds in his mouth, balances a ball on top of a stick held in his mouth and spins it in the air according to the movements of his head. At the end of the series of exercises, Rastelli smiles with satisfaction, and his personality and good humor is contagious. His small dance passes and his poses might well sell his act even if they were carried out with less precision. Holding a ball on his knee, Rastelli throws it up, does a somersault and catches it in the same place. He bounces two balls on his head at the same time, juggles with four sticks, two by two, juggles with eight plates and carries out a variety of other exercises with an indescribable speed. He then goes into a handstand on one hand, on a piece of equipment that looks like an upside-down coffee machine, and at the same time spins a pole with his feet. With a blindfold he carries out, on a piece of equipment looking like a lamp, a head balance and at the same time juggles with sticks and spins a pole with his feet, all this while the apparatus spins itself around. This is an extraordinary example of what one can achieve supporting skill with infinite patience and daily training. For the finale, a blue and silver piece of apparatus is brought on stage, illuminated from the inside with electric lights and decorated with bulbs and a pair of American flags. Sitting on a seat, Rastelli spins a large five-pointed star with one of his feet, while the other spins a ring,

ENRICO RASTELLI

ENRICO RASTELLI

with his upper limbs he juggles with three sticks. A highly spectacular feat that provoked the passion of the public, making Rastelli return many times for applause."[17]

In June of 1924, he performed at Hennepin-Orpheum, in Minneapolis, and a critic of the local paper wrote: "If Enrico Rastelli isn't the world's greatest juggler, he is surely the best showman amongst those who earn their living balancing long poles on their forehead. He is surely the best juggler ever to be seen in years."[18] A month later in San Francisco they wrote about him: "On the billboard he appears as the world's greatest juggler. And after having seen him we are ready to confirm such a title. It is the most extraordinary act of this generation that we have seen in 25 years. Don't have the courage to miss him!"[19] In another daily newspaper the critics were yet more indicative: "It is quite unusual that a juggler has a good place on the billboard at the Orpheum. Usually jugglers, acrobats and acts of this type are used to open and close the program and have relative importance."

On the program it was written:

Unique and Extraordinary

ENRICO RASTELLI

"The Master Juggler of the World"

One of the ingredients that allowed him to have an immediate hold on the American public was his incredible speed. Before him the jugglers, wrapped up in evening jackets or in Prussian army uniforms, presented complicated feats and moved carts, cannons, and horses with a sluggishness that in our eyes would seem exasperating. In 1928, Rastelli returned for the last time to America, and with the notorious crisis of 1929, there weren't many reasons for the juggler to do further American tours. In 1925, Rastelli was, however, discovered by the German public, who didn't lack affection, consensus, and good contracts.

In January of 1925, the European city with the greatest number of variety theatres and with a competent and enthusiastic public was Berlin. The agent Paul Spadoni, in the past a great juggler who in 1928 had opened an artistic agency in that city, had been trying for a while to convince the management of the Wintergarten to sign up Rastelli. That theatre was born in 1888, on the wave of success that had already been given to entertainment halls such as Walhalla and Alhambra, but the Wintergarten, "the Theatre of the Starred Sky," so-called for the characteristic blue ceiling dotted with myriad tiny lights, had become in a short time the best place for the Berliners to look for entertainment.[20]

From its opening it had, therefore, hosted the best variety artists of that epoch: from Harry Houdini to Loie Fuller, from Cleo de Merode to the comedian Otto Reutter, from the trapeze artist Codona to Grock, who performed accompanied by a splendid 32-piece orchestra conducted by the maestro Paul Lincke. Furthermore at the Wintergarten, the best jugglers in the last 40 years had passed by: Paul Cinquevalli, Salerno, Kara, and Spadoni himself.

On April 1, 1925, Enrico Rastelli debuted at the Wintergarten. He was an unexpected triumph without precedent. Barely three days after the debut, the theatre management drew up a new contract for August of that same year, with a pay raise to 16,000 marks a month, plus travel expenses for the artists and equipment. Never before, or since, had the press taken such as interest in a juggler. There is a photo of Rastelli, taken in front of a hoard of photographers wanting him in every pose: with a newspaper between his hands, serious, smiling, still, at work. Soon all the reporters went to look for him in his hotel, asking him to pose with his family, at the table, in the car, even in the bathtub—just as happens to famous people today.

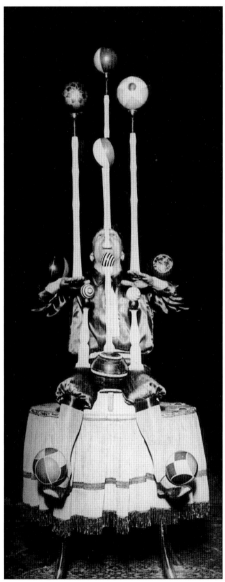

Additionally, he started receiving offers from businesses that wanted to sponsor his shows: manufacturers of razor blades, typewriters, shoes, clothes and more. Poems, drawings, caricatures, special editions of magazines and anything else that could honor the talent of an artist in those years were dedicated to him. Above all the things that most struck the German public was his speed, his grace, and the incredible variety of feats that he offered. The Italian names evoked a close exoticism in distance, but not so close in terms of life and art.

In brief, a Rastelli-mania exploded in Berlin that drove all German spectators to queue up for days to buy tickets to see his shows. Enrico Rastelli had by then learned to make the most of the huge work demand to manage his occupation in the best way: canceling, modifying, and adding clauses to contracts that were signed with an astonishing frequency. With a pen he inserted extra expenses that he

RASTELLI IN A TWELVE PIECE BALANCE

would take for eventual afternoon shows; he required his name on the billboard and decided his own position in the line-up. He even, notwithstanding, pre-printed contracts stating that rehearsals could only be carried out during certain times, obtained special lighting so he was able to train at all hours. During his entire career he never stopped training at least eight hours a day.

Even with the highest pay, the most comfortable changing room, his name written in the biggest letters, the best stage entrance, despite all of this he was always looked up to

RASTELLI JUGGLING SIX PLATES WHILE BOUNCING A BALL ON HIS FOREHEAD

by his colleagues. He was a so-called "artist for the artists," who was even admired by the other components of the cast, who ran to peek between the curtains to see his act. After the rehearsals, he entertained other jugglers, who often came to visit him. He was a prodigy of suggestions; and he explained how to build props and he gave away those props he no longer needed. It wasn't only the spectators and the other artists that ran to admire him. In Berlin, it was also usual for all the managers of the European variety theatres to visit him, who then proposed the best deals to the best artists.

From that moment on, it was a continual follow up of successes in the major German and European cities: Frankfort, Hamburg, Nüremberg, Stuttgart, Düsseldorf, Cologne, Hanover, Budapest, Copenhagen, Vienna, Zürich and many others. His art started to attract the attention of the intellectuals. Among the many admirers who went to greet him in his changing room, one of the more frequent visitors was Oskar Schlemmer, director of Bauhaus, who found in the corporeity of the juggler an important backup in his theory of the actor, so much so as to insert some of the exercises in the training of his theatre pupils.

In those years, notwithstanding the budding of his success, he had conserved the simplicity and the common sense typical of village people: "My life changes little. For 11 months a year, I travel with my wife and a young cousin, and for one month a year we stay at Bergamo, at my parents place, where my children live."[21]

And yet at a certain point, he felt the need to drastically change his act. Another popular entertainment form for the people, other than the cinema, that was attracting the masses —sport. Many jugglers had already inserted sporting equipment and techniques of the more popular activities into their act. For his new routine, Rastelli decided to use soccer as his inspiration. On August 1, 1930, he debuted with his new juggling-soccer routine at the Apollo Theatre in Düsseldorf. For his creation he used costumes and scenery that transformed the stage into a soccer field. He added new tricks to his old repertoire, all very spectacular, and all carried out with sewn-leather balls. At the end of his act he invited spectators to come on stage to re-enact a soccer game in which he was more often than not the winner, given that the poor goalkeepers weren't able to deflect even one of the throws that he booted while performing spectacular somersaults.

If he had huge success with this act it probably depended on the large popularity of soccer, which had become one of the most-followed sports in Europe. The historian Le Grand-Chabrière wrote: "If juggling were a sport, Rastelli would beat every record. Facing this artist we had a feeling similar to that which we experience when we recognize a sporting champion able to develop might and dexterity of man."[22] Owing to this new style of juggling, his already high publicity earnings were augmented by the sponsorship of an important soccer equipment manufacturer, Kaspar Berg, in Nüremberg.[23]

Choosing to become a juggling-athlete, Rastelli made himself (even if unconsciously) assigned to some modern theories of the actor. The juggler, as the acrobat, is an artistic figure that places himself half way between an athlete and an actor. The need for absolute precision of

RASTELLI BALANCING SOCCER BALLS

the manipulated objects reminds us of the gesture of many sportsmen. The possibility of error in the gesture places the juggler between the dexterity of the body and in some way ties him to the techniques of reciting. Franco Ruffino, in his *Teatro e boxe* (*Theatre and Boxing*), makes the paragon between the credibility of the body of a boxer and that of an actor, the gestures not being limited to a copy of the boxer.[24] It must be real and show how this "accurateness" of the actor was the center of the work of many people in the theatre in the first decade of the 1900's.

Among these was Artaud, who defined the actor as an "actor of the heart," forced to deal with physical obstacles opposing his body, just like a juggler. Around the same years, the lightweight boxer Georges Carpentier reaped his first important victories—ending the domination of the powerful heavyweights—with his agility. In return, he received

ENRICO RASTELLI

tremendous support from fans. Carpentier inter-preted the hidden need of the majority of the con-sumers of that time who wanted to admire dexterity and elegance more than just brute force.[25] Rastelli, as was Carpentier, described by Ruffini, sanctioned the removal of the strongmen jugglers (huge mass-es of muscles with clumsy movements) from the cir-cus and the stage and introduced slim, able, aware and smiling athletes.

One of the most sensitive cities of Enrico Rastelli's art was Paris, which in those years, had the unchallenged position as the capital of the perma-nent circuses.[26] Rastelli had made his debut in December of 1921, at the Alhambra, in one of his first good contracts. Then in May of 1925, he was at the Empire, the managers of which—Dufrenne and Varna—had to pay him 1800 francs a day, more than double that of the time before. The Empire was a "circus-music hall" which had a form similar to that of the theatre, with a large stage and with an arena out front.[27] There was even a pit for a 30-piece orchestra. It was a well-frequented place, which paid great attention to the quality of the per-formances. Dufrenne and Varna at that time insert-ed a clause into the contracts of performers that was tied to the outcome of their exhibitions—in case of evident displeasure on behalf of the audience, the management had the right to withdraw the contract without owing any-thing to the artist.[28]

Rastelli's true triumph came on his return to Paris when he was hired in the prestigious (and permanent) Medrano Circus in October of 1930, where he performed 40-minute shows.

All the Parisian artists and intellectuals were fascinated by Enrico Rastelli's art. Colette, the great French writer, was also a variety artist in her youth, and she wrote: "Rastelli, while he juggles with a galaxy of planets, seems transported by them, mixed up in their orbits, sucked up into space." Cocteau defined Rastelli as one of the three great modern circus artists, together with the masked Barbette and the Australian ropewalker, Con Colleano. Visiting Rastelli in his dressing room were Sacha Guitry, the poet Jaques Feschotte, the pianist Edwin Fischer and who knows who else.

Rastelli had in fact become a symbol of a juggling genius. He had taken out any trace of a plot, which was fashionable between jugglers of that time, and he had returned to the

simplicity of the medieval jugglers, to such a great extent that he deprived his performance of meaning that was to be able to be interpreted infinitely. The intellectuals of that
time read into his act an open work interpreting on their own will and often giving an
impromptu meaning that it would only have had in part.[29] Briefly, the circuit that he had
entered made him part of a special romantic category, a bit like what had happened to the
clown figure, who in those years became essentially a sad clown. Vito Pandolfi, in his
Anthology of a Great Actor, left us the following interesting and profound reflection:

"The Italian tradition, while it had worn out its main thread—that of the theatre of the
modern drama—on one side created great actors and great authors for the music halls and
for the circus. On the other hand, there was the more genuine part of their cinematic productions. The connections are rather close. Fratellini, Rastelli and Toto inherited and
developed performance forms at times, the seeds of which are clearly owed to mime
games, musicals, customs, and comici dell'arte. The tradition, with its revelations and its
terms for the great Italian actor, has directly reached these expressions."[30]

At the end of the month of November 1931, during a performance at the Apollo Theatre
in Nüremberg, Rastelli, as he had been doing for some
time in his soccer act, threw balls at the spectators,
who had to re-throw them to him, making Rastelli
catch them in all sorts of different positions. One of
these spectators threw the ball with excessive vio-
lence, whipping the stick out of his mouth, which he
had held between his teeth and on which the sphere
should have been caught. In this way, he slightly cut
the roof of his mouth that started a slight hemorrhage.
(It seems unfortunate, however, that Rastelli should
suffer a type of congenital hemophilia that had already
caused problems in the past.) From that slight graze he
began losing a copious amount of blood, which also
continued during the trip that would have taken the
Rastellis to their home in Bergamo.

Notwithstanding the increase in the poor conditions of his health, the juggler didn't want to suspend
nor put off the ambitious project that he had been
preparing for some time: an Italian tour that would
have finally given him the chance to return to his
native country and to make the art that had made him
famous in the whole world known to his fellow countrymen. It was all perfectly organized. The company's
plan was trusted to the then-most powerful theatrical

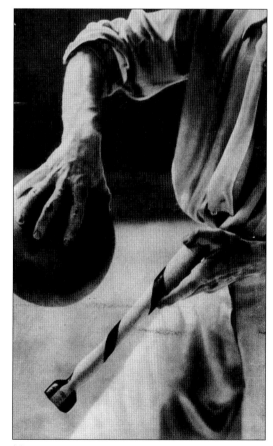

THE HANDS OF RASTELLI

100 YEAR POSTER OF ENRICO RASTELLI

firm in Italy—Suvini-Zerboni. The project had a trial run in Rastelli's city for five performances in four days. Rastelli had a great power of choice for the program's line-up. With the exception of Grock, who anyway had a house in Imperia, and Italian artists such as Fregoli or Petrolini, there were no other stars of the international variety performing in Italy with regular frequency.[31]

The Italian audiences were used to a show that derived from the caffè concert with the prevalence of eccentrics and singers—not acrobats and jugglers. Therefore, Rastelli's invention went unobserved during his tour and was wasted on the Italian variety, or he may have had modified his way of doing light entertainment with the consequent influence on the theatrical world that, in those years, gave due credit to the antique and "refined" physical arts which the juggler brought to bear.

Rastelli didn't have a place in the syndicate, nor did he receive contributions from the state. He was completely on the margin, an independent artist, a bit like Toto in Italy, engaged in making his way, with his own strength, using what was then a complicated mechanism.[32] And yet the organization of his future Italian tour was trusted to the Suvini-Zerboni company, which had already in 1916 formed, with Giuseppe Paradossi and the Chiarelli brothers, an influential society for the management of the major Italian halls.[33] The entrance of the Suvini-Zerboni, which in 1939-40 was produced and directed by Cesare and written by Benito Mussolini and Gioacchino Forzano, received abundant and extraordinary financing, which lets us envisage the exploitation of Rastelli's image for some time in favor of propaganda for the regime, which was then in its inception.[34]

If Rastelli had lived longer, fascism would have been able to hold him up to signify the virtues and power of the human being, a model of Italianism in the 1920's, exported and admired in the whole world with an exemplary private sphere of three children with a healthy life dedicated to his work. Moreover, he had become a "sports-artist" and we know the importance that the regime attributed in those years to sport and particularly to soccer. However, no one was ever able to verify this: the evening show of December 6, at Duse, was the last time that Rastelli's body expressed all the energy that had stupefied thousands of spectators throughout the whole world. That same day, in the afternoon, Professor Minelli—first doctor in Bergamo—seeing the poor condition of Rastelli's health, strongly advised against his performing that evening. Rastelli, however, didn't wish to stop due to his pride. He worked, with the end result creating a worsening of his state of health. The night between December 12 and 13, the hemorrhage ended his life at the age of 34. The news of his death echoed around the world, transmitted via radio and reported in daily papers.

On December 15, a vast crowd followed Rastelli's coffin as his funeral procession moved through Bergamo's streets, past the Teatro Eleonora Duse, where his last performance had taken place, toward the cemetery at the foot of the mountains. Whole streets had to be cordoned off to enable the ceremony to go on without interruption. The artist's final resting place is a magnificent, marble mausoleum with a life-sized statue of the juggler standing with three balls—one foot atop one ball, one ball held in his left hand and a third ball on an upraised index finger of the right hand. The epitaph inscribed on the tomb reads:

Enrico Rastelli
Insuperato Signore Delle Leggi Dell Equilibrio
Acclamato In Tutti I Paesi Del Mondo
Conobbe Sopra Tutto E Serbo Fedelta
Alle Supreme Leggi Dell Amore Cristiano
E Qui Attende
La Resurrezione Finale

English Translation:
Enrico Rastelli
Unsurpassed master of the laws of equilibrium
Acclaimed in every country in the world
Unsurpassed—and conquered only in death

Inscribed on the pedestal beneath the statue of Rastelli:
Insuperabile Invitto Artista
Vinto Sol Da Morte

Many things have been written about Rastelli since his death; some of the tales have been exaggerated, and not everything, especially from his earlier days, can be proved. It was at first speculated that his death may have resulted from an abscess caused by a splinter from his mouthstick. However, according to the doctors, Rastelli had, unknown to himself and his family, been close to death for a long time. It was only his incomparable energy that enabled him, on repeated occasions, to overcome the congenital weakness of his body. His condition was exacerbated by his unrelenting training schedule and by the strain of touring. Despite his strenuous work, he always felt fit. But in the final weeks

HENRIETTE RASTELLI & KARL-HEINZ ZIETHEN
WITH ENRICO RASTELLI STATUE, MILAN 1974

before his death troubling signs began to emerge. Whenever he bumped himself or even merely leaned against something, bruises appeared. His anemia developed in hyperemia. The bleeding gums in Nüremberg were one of the last warnings.

All good jugglers have a special disposition for their craft, and Rastelli's great talent was his ability to toss and catch. Rastelli also had an extraordinary ability to juggle with different kinds of objects. His repertory embodied many separate, unique achievements, such as juggling with eight and 10 balls, or juggling with eight sticks, or six sticks while balancing an object on his head, or five sticks and a ball, or six torches. The list goes on and on: he could juggle with eight disks while balancing an object on his head, or juggle six plates while bouncing a ball on his forehead. Another extraordinary achievement was the tossing of six disks while skipping rope and keeping a ring rotating around his foot. He primarily juggled with even numbers of objects (four, six, eight, or 10), most often thrown and caught simultaneously in pairs. Apparently, though, he did perform some tricks with five objects (three with one hand, two with the other) as well as a cascade with three sticks.

Rastelli was also a master of various equilibristic juggling tricks. While doing a one-armed handstand with his right hand, he could rotate a rod with his feet, balance a lamp on his head, and rotate a plate on a mouthstick while juggling two balls with his left hand. Standing on his head and spinning rings on his legs, he could simultaneously juggle with three balls. While lying on a cushion he could use one foot to rotate a chair (whose legs pointed upwards), spin a ring around his other leg, spin a bowl on a mouthstick, and at the same time juggle with three sticks or, sometimes, four balls.

His cousin, Umberto Schichtholz-Bedini, and his wife were not only his assistants on the stage, but also his closest aides in private life, and it was they who managed his business affairs. Enrico Rastelli had no time for anything other than his work and his family. even his close friends saw him only during his daily practice sessions. His wife, Henriette was always responsible for getting things ready before a performance. Whenever they arrived at a new venue, it was she who took charge of adjusting the lights, while Rico, as she called Rastelli, would already be rehearsing on stage. He was also a real fanatic about his art, never satisfied with what he had already achieved and always eager—even when he had reached the pinnacle of his career—to devote several hours each day to practicing his art. Enrico Rastelli's skills raised juggling to a new plane, and set the standards by which all jugglers came to be measured. His name can be found in all the major encyclopedias, a privilege shared by very few performing artists.

ENRICO RASTELLI'S SUCCESSORS

I f the Italian culture had adequately valued the circus arts, Rastelli would occupy a place in the history of the Italian show between Scarpetta and Petrolini. If he had been born in France they would have spoken about him as if he was the one who had continued the art and sensitivity that Carnè had magically brought back to life in *Les enfants du paradis.* We refer to his fortune and to the influence that he had over the work of jugglers and those who followed him. Already, during his last few years of life, his fame caused many impersonators to try to make their way using his style and his technique. After his death, there was an acceleration of this process and the number of jugglers who tried to copy the great master increased.

Serafino Ivanoff was a colleague at the many rehearsals and few games of the young Enrico. He had left the Rastellis in 1919, after the start of the Russian Revolution, when they returned to Italy. Even when he was on his own, he hadn't stopped training and he was able to create an act very similar to that of his more famous rehearsal partner. One of his contemporaries, and fellow countrymen of comparable status, was Serge "Flash" Formitschew, born in Russia and adopted by the Andos Troupe and His Six Japs, from whom he learned the art of juggling and who, in America, obtained great success close to that of Rastelli. He married the cinema star Belly Kickbridge, thanks to whom he was able to enter into the mundane Hollywood scene and he was the first juggler to appear in an elegant ice show before his death in 1956.

MASSIMILIANO TRUZZI

Another great juggler in Rastelli's style was the offspring of a great Italian circus family, Massimiliano Truzzi, born in Poland in 1903. After Rastelli had adopted the stage entrance in a Japanese kimono, Truzzi, not wanting to appear less exotic, chose an Indian costume that he changed at the end of his career for a Spanish one. Truzzi also made speed one of his winning points—he was able to juggle three soccer balls with his head and in 1940 was the first juggler who was allowed to perform at the central ring of the Ringling Bros. and Barnum & Bailey Circus.

During his first tour of the United States in 1923, Rastelli had worked alongside the Pickelmann acrobats in the same show. He saw the juggling rehearsals of the young Paul to whom he suggested to continue training. Paul Pickelmann had taken the stage name of Paolo Piletto and had such success he was nicknamed the "German Rastelli." In 1929, he performed at the Cirque d'Hiver in Paris—he also bounced three soccer balls on his head. When Rastelli died, Paolo Piletto took his inheritance, becoming the principle attraction in Europe's variety theatres. Paolo Bedini-Tafani, born in 1914, was a nephew of Rastelli and at the age of 14 was so impressed by his uncle's act that he decided to take the same road.[35]

BOB RIPA

Bob Ripa

Several women adopted Rastelli's style, making it more feminine. In 1933, the juggler Trixie, born in Budapest, performed at the Medrano Circus in Paris and, at barely 12 years old, was already compared to the great juggler. Later on, she appeared in the film *Broadway Melody* in which the main actor was Fred Astaire. Another of Rastelli's imitators was Angelo Picinelli, son of the equilibrist Fulvio, who had introduced rings into his act rather than plates. Owing to his considerable stature, he was able to carry out exercises that took on an unusual form, such as when he juggled with four sticks "Rastelli style," two in each hand, and they seemed to dance on their own. Another Italian, Italo Medini, whose father was a good friend of the great juggler, had often watched Rastelli practice and had at an early age tried to copy his style. Danish juggler Bob Ripa was every bit as good as his older contemporaries. He died heroically at the age of 31 in 1944, killed in a plane crash in the Pacific Ocean while traveling to entertain American troops.

Freddy Zay was called the "Rastelli of the High Unicycle." The most appreciated moment of his show was when he balanced a billiard cue on his forehead with an abattoir on the summit, while he spun a ring on his foot and juggled six with his hands. He became the manager of the Apollo in Nüremberg, another beautiful variety theatre that unfortunately doesn't exist any longer. Eight years after Rastelli had created his soccer match act, Jean Florian and Hermann Matthe created an act in which they demonstrated their soccer skills. The artists mentioned are only a few of those who, taking their ideas from the innovations of Rastelli, substantially changed the entire world of jugglers in the 1920's and 1930's. Unfortunately, however, after the death of the Italian artist, such an increase in quantity didn't correspond to an increase in public interest, which started to desert the circus and the variety.

At the start of World War II, athletic and physical ability became incorporated into modern sports, which guaranteed a major influence and a major variety in the performances. The stage performances were, however, collected by the cinema, which initially through the magician George Melies and then through others absorbed the entire brilliant finds of the variety onto the silver screen.

The circus and the variety were the performance forms most hit by the effects of World War II. Numerous permanent circuses and variety theatres were completely destroyed by bombing. Furthermore, following the great conflict, the development

FREDDY ZAY

of communications and industrial activities underwent such a fast growth that all the spectators had a different philosophy on life and, therefore, a different attitude with regard to the performances. These were the years of the triumph of the cinema, the years in which the sports-show took ever more of a foothold the world over.

The circus and the variety theatre, like that which had happened to the stage show before and the introductory variety after, started to be more and more neglected by the

HERMANN MATTHE

GILBERTO ZAVATTA

public and the mass media. Between the two genuses, the variety theatres suffered the most. The circus was, in fact, able to survive. Owing to the belligerent character of the people used to a thousand daily battles to survive and, above all, due to the emphasis of the type of traveling shows that allowed the big tops to rise, for a certain period of time, anywhere there may have been even a minimum earning.

The Italian circus thus experienced, up until the 1960's, a difficult period of crisis until, alongside the economic boom, they were busy with gigantic productions which were truly colossal with a return of a slight hint of pantomime. It was the same for other European countries: France, Spain, Germany, and England continued to be places where the circus managers had to battle on a daily basis to compete for a small slice of the market. The other continents weren't able to offer a comfortable refuge either. Asia and Africa didn't hire artists, even if there were destinations for tours, while Australia had few interesting complexes; a scarce population and the distances between habitations almost prohibited the development of traveling complexes.

In the United States, show business had taken other routes. The only circus complex able to offer good contracts was the Ringling Bros. and the Barnum & Bailey Circus which, however, chose only the best jugglers, leaving the others out of the circuit. In brief, the international panorama was desolate. While only a dozen years before, a good name on the billboard guaranteed a full house of festive spectators; but now the public didn't recognize the circus and variety artists anymore, apart from some exceptions who became evermore uncommon. Whereas in the Golden Age of variety, Cinquevalli or Rastelli, like the talents in other disciplines, they appeared in the same program as Sarah Bernhardt and Josephine Baker.

After the war the jugglers returned to the anonymity they had been in up to two centuries beforehand and, unfortunately, also started to be neglected by the group of cultured men who had such consideration for them in the years between the two great wars. In short, for over a century, the career of the juggler had appeared more interesting and enumerative than others, while in the late 50's the instability and uncertainty returned to be among the principle components of the profession.

In the second post-war period the most predominant props were clubs that had substituted the sticks, balls of various dimensions and rings, while the style remained that of Rastelli—fast and essential. For the troupes that continued to exist, it was the wage of only one act that would be enough for the whole family, often numerous and in continual growth. The growth of the crisis brought a swift drop in the group acts and forced the ex-components of the troupes to create acts in duos or as individual artists, thus increasing the total number of acts in circulation and starting a chaos that brought a further inflation of the market. With many jugglers in circulation to be able to guarantee a certain quantity of work, one needed to be in a level above that of the average and many Italians were able to continue to work on the leftovers of Rastelli's repertory.

Among these, Maurizio Bonaccorso, Giancarlo Madera, Daviso Martini, Danglar Rossante, and Mimmo Veneziano, all talented jugglers on the wire. Additionally, making names for themselves were Sergio Chiesa and Eduardo Raspini, the latter of whom was gifted with enormous charm and stage presence and had an appealing physique that earned him the name, "Don Giovanni of the Jugglers." Then there were Gilberto Zavatta, Nando, Paolo and Mauro Orfei, with a more traditional style, the elegant Luciano Bello, who juggled on the free ladder and the virtuous Alberto Sforzi, who was able to

SERGIO CHIESA

ALEGRIA BROTHERS

RUDY CARDENAS

ERNEST MONTEGO

perform many great exploits, such as juggling 10 rings while balancing on a rope. Another noted Italian was Benito "Nino" Frediani, born in 1940 in Lisbon but who came from a great family of equestrian acrobats famous for their never-equaled triple-column horseback. Nino had a strong comic component that allowed him to win over the public at Las Vegas.

An artist who gave new flavor to the traditional Rastelli style was Rudy Cardenas. Born in 1931 in Guadalajara, and coming from a Suarez family—the owner of many circuses in South America—Cardenas obtained a contract in 1947 in Cuba where fate had it he was noticed by an agent who signed him up for a circuit of the Paramount Theatre Corporation, which was already in decline. In 1955, he performed in a European tour with the acrobatic basketball players, the Harlem Globetrotters. From 1974, the managers of the Lido hired him and they had him performing, every now and again, in the Parisian and Las Vegas venues. His main secret was his South American rhythm and from this was

MICHAEL CHIRRICK

TON WELLS

borne an American/Hispanic style that centered around dynamism and frenetic speed, juggling with clubs, balls, rings, and sombreros divided up with fast somersaults. In this genre, the Alegria Brothers, known also as the D'Angolys from the Spanish Briatore family demonstrated increasible ball manipulation, as well as fast club-passing.

Ernest Montego, from Germany, the half-brother of Francis and Lottie Brunn, played in 1959 the lead role in the revue *A Ball Rolls Round the World*, which traced the life story of Enrico Rastelli, performed at the Friedrichstadt Palast in Berlin, Germany. Another relative of the Brunn family who performs in the Rastelli style is Michael Chirrick. His mother, Lottie Brunn, became in 1951 the most successful and fastest female juggler in the world. A delightful juggler with soccer balls in the '50s was Ton Wells from Germany. He did not work with the usual large soccer balls exclusively—much more difficult because they are so unwieldy. Ton Well's greatest achievement came in 1955, when he appeared in the German film *Reaching for the Stars*, which tells a story of a

RAPHAEL DE CARLOS

KOSEN KAGAMI

juggler who lives only for his work. In Ton's footsteps followed Raphael de Carlos, from Cuba, who graduated from the Cuban National Circus School in Havana in 1986. He specializes in soccer balls, but he can also juggle up to seven small balls.

The work of Kosen Kagami, from Tokyo, Japan, reflects the spirit of traditional Japanese juggling. Performing for the last 45 years, he is one of the last artists to work with two handsticks and a ball and one of the last to dress in a traditional kimono and hakama (a pleated skirt worn over the kimono). Today, Kagami has several pupils. They accompany the master on all his journeys and performances; and they assist him and learn from him the techniques of juggling and the meanings of the props and movements, which have remained unchanged for centuries. Masahiro Mizuno and Kenzaburo Ishikawa have performed ancient Japanese tricks since 1998.

JUGGLERS WITH BALLS, CLUBS AND RINGS

RUDY HORN

One of the greatest technical jugglers with balls, clubs and rings was Rudy Horn, born in Germany. He gave his first solo performance at the age of nine. Horn was a superlative juggler with five balls. He showed his audiences a long run of back crosses, as well as juggling the five above his head. He was able to juggle nine balls but never did perform it. In 1965, in Las Vegas, Rudy Horn managed to juggle with seven rings for one minute and five seconds, making 250 throws. he also introduced special effects to liven up his act. He created a routine using five lighted balls, something that he had never seen done before. A brilliant trick of his was also bouncing seven balls against a concert drum set at an angle on the floor in front of him. In another trick he tossed a teaspoon from his foot to his forehead, where he balanced it in a vertical position, bowl upward. He gave a slight nod with his head, and the spoon ended up behind his ear. Horn's finale was the trick for which he is best known—kicking six tea cups and saucers from his foot onto the top of his head, one at a time while idling on a high unicycle.

Fast club jugglers who made a name for themselves in the mid-1960's were Pepito Alvarez (from Spain), Nino Frediani (from Italy), Sandro Briatore (from Spain), and Tony Ferco (from Czech Republic). In the 1970's, there was Suzanne and Fudi (from Hungary), Steve Bor (from Australia), George Sollveno (from Switzerland), Victor Ponce (from Argentina), and Wally Eastwood (from the United States). In club juggling, an innovation that has become particularly popular in recent years is "footwork": the juggler catches a club on the top of his foot, then kicks it back up into the juggle. The first solo juggler to incorporate this new style into his act was the Spaniard Ugo Garrido in 1960. Twenty years later, Spaniard Manuel Alvarez invented many new "kickup" variations using three clubs. In his finale trick he "boomerangs" up to seven plastic plates over an audience—keeping them in the air by tossing and catching them in sequence as they return.

MANUEL ALVAREZ

As previous chapters have shown, virtually every genre of juggling has produced some outstanding female performers. And there were a few excellent female jugglers in the 1970's—including Eva Vida and Gipsy Gruss, who have risen to the very heights of the juggling profession and they have been every bit as influential in the development of the juggling art as their male counterparts. Gipsy Gruss, for instance, comes from a well-known French circus family, the Bougliones. She made her debut as a rope dancer at the age of 12. In the mid-1960's, she appeared for the first time as a juggler under the name Dionni Wolls. Gipsy's marriage to Alexis Gruss brought together two great circus families. Gipsy Gruss trained her son Stephane in the early-1980's and performed various juggling acts with him, including club and ring passing. The most glamorous female juggler to come from Hungary was Eva Vida. As a young girl, she attended ballet classes and after that she spent six years at the Hungarian State Circus School in Budapest, where she obtained her final diploma in 1959.

GIPSY GRUSS

WILLI BALLADINI

EVA VIDA

The first American solo juggler to rise to fame in the early-1970's was Albert Lucas. He has a long-running relationship with world records, and has appeared several times in noted publications for his achievements with high numbers of balls and rings juggled. Albert Lucas tied a Guinness record when he flashed twelve rings in 1996, and was the first person ever to flash 13 rings in 2002. He is the founder of the International Sport Juggling Federation. Albert's younger brother, David Lee (Moreira), made his first appearance at age three in his brother's act with the Ice Capades. Among the new generation of American jugglers belongs Dick Franco, Barrett Felker, and Mark Nizer.

JUGGLING SPECIALTIES

In 1940, Willi Balladini created "mouth juggling" in which the instrument of propulsion for the balls was the mouth—this act had great success and many impersonators. The most extraordinary perhaps was Gran Picaso, born in 1938 in Valencia, where he trained as

CASTORS

a torero but ended up playing the trumpet in the orchestra of a circus. This was an important step in his life, which allowed him to understand what his true vocation was. He
became the first juggler to juggle six balls with his mouth, usually ping-pong balls. Gran
Picaso started his career at 27, fairly old compared to the norm but, nevertheless, reached
such levels as to be hired by the Ringling Bros. and Barnum & Bailey Circus and then onto
the major showrooms of Las Vegas. Rod Laver, from England, is also a specialist in ping-
pong ballwork. He has juggled since 2001 up to eight balls, using his mouth and hands (and
juggling four balls with his mouth alone). He also spits the balls against the wall to bounce
back to him, and works with a mechanical prop resembling a face, which will spit ping-
pong balls for Rod to catch. Another unique routine with ping-pong balls is performed by
American Jeff Taveggian, known as the "Paddleman." His routine involves trolling ping-
pong balls between nine paddles, attached to almost every body part.

One of the most outstanding equilibristic jugglers in the mid-1950's was Spaniard Tito
Reyes. He juggled clubs and rings with his hands and feet while he performed a headstand
on a podium. Reyes also taught foot-juggling to his daughter, Consuela, and his son,

Rudolfo. Achievement and originality brought the Three Castors (Eddy, Charly, Toly) and Jean Claude, all from France, to the forefront of foot-juggling. The Bulgarian performer Angel Bojiloff, during the 1960's, was juggling with balls and rings while lying on his back on a slack-wire. Bert Holt, from Germany, presented a very strange juggling act in which he swung from a rope that he gripped with his teeth.

ALBERT LUCAS

ANGEL BOJILOFF

FREDY & MARIO BEROUSEK

DR. HOT & NEON

GRAN PICASO

*SORIN MUNTEANUS & CONSUELA REYES AT REHEARSAL,
CIRCUS WILL HAGENBECK (GERMANY) 1975*

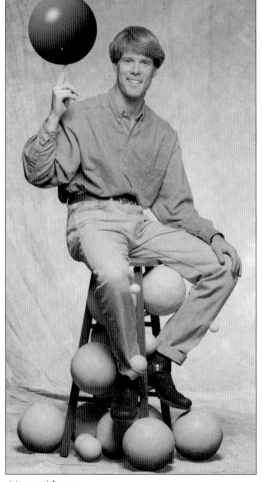

MARK NIZER

---

1 *Berliner Tageblatt*, 1927, Pandolfi, Vito, *Antologia del grande attore*, Bari, Laterza, 1954, p. 511.

2 *Scherl Magazine*, 1928, Pandolfi, Vito, *Antologia del grande attore*, Bari, Laterza, 1954, p. 512.

3 The Talon Law, enacted in 1873 in France, forbade work for children less than 15 years to perform alone and up to 12 if together with their parents.

4 De Goncourt had described such acts: "...this overlaying of two juggling styles melted into one and created bizarre and unexpected games." op. cit. p. 72.

5 From the *Programme* of the Alhambra Hall, December 1921-January 1922.

6 London Theatres of Varieties, Ltd.

7 Only in Russia the state directives already then forced the performances to have a logical thread, similar to what we have taken on in our musicals nowadays. Ciofi, Atti, Fabio, Ferretti, Daniela, *Russia: 1900-1930 L'arte della Scena*, Milano, Electa, 1990.

8 For the intense activity in the animal cages in those years see: Hagenbeck, Carlo, *Io e le belve*, Milano, Quintieri, 1910.

9 The trade embargo stopped in 1924.

10 Contract with Bertram Mills.

11 At the opening night of the RCVP Paul Cinquevalli had taken part. Delfont, Bernard, *Curtain Up! The Story Of the Royal Variety Performance*, London, Robson Books, 1989.

12 *The Era*, January 25, 1923.

13 *The Era*, February 1, 1923.

14 Found at the London Theatre Museum—Research Collection.

15 Part of the E.F. Albee Collection, at the Special Collections and Manuscripts Library at the University of Iowa. We thank A. McCown for the note.

SANDRO FROM THE ALEGRIA BROTHERS TRIO

16 The palace was converted into a cinema in 1932 and in 1950 it returned to hosting live concerts. In 1966 it finally returned to its original title to be considered a legitimate Broadway theatre.

17 *Billboard*, April 21, 1923.

18 *Minneapolis Journal*, June 30, 1924.

19 *San Francisco Call and Post*, July 14, 1924.

20 The scenographic effects at that time have cost a noteworthy sum.

21 *Scherl Magazine*, 1928, Pandolfi, op. cit.

22 Le Grand-Chabrier, Pierre Paret.

23 Cartolina publications and letters from Kasper Berg.

24 Ruffini, Franco, *Teatro e boxe*, Bologna, Il Mulino, 1994.

25 Ruffini, Franco, *op. cit.*

26 Adrian, *Histoire Illustrée des cirques parisiens*, Adrian, Paris, 1957.

27 The contract stated "to expect to work indistinctly in the ring or on stage."

28 Another clause in the contract stated "that the artist had to hand over the complete musical score for the orchestra. In the case that the score was incomplete or badly written, the corrections were charged to the artist."

29 Pandolfi, Vito, *Antologia del grande attore*, Bari, Laterza, 1954, p. 503.

30 Morosi, Antonio, *Il teatro di varietà in Italia*, Calvetti, Firenze, 1901.

31 Meldolesi, Claudio, *Fra Toto e Gadda, sei invenzioni sprecate dal teatro italiano*, Roma, Bulzoni, 1987.

32 Pedullà, Gianfranco, *Il teatro italiano nel tempo del fascismo*, Bologna, Il Mulino, 1994.

33 Cesare was the last in a trilogy for the two actors that also included the *Campo di Maggio* and *Villafranca*.

34 Definitions by Legrand-Chabrier in Adrian, 1977, op. cit.

VI

OUTSTANDING JUGGLERS

THE MAJOR FAMILIES

Despite the period of crisis and the escalation of genre and sub-genre, there were a few artists—extremely rare cases—who reached such high levels that they seemed almost wasted in an age of general disinterest towards juggling. Among these exponents were four great families: Bob Bramson; Francis Brunn; Bela and Kris Kremo; and Anthony Gatto.

Bob Bramson was the most-talented representative of hoop juggling. These particular props, which for many years were largely used as a child's toy, have the distinction of not only their ability to be thrown in the air but also to be rolled on a smooth surface. The first movement learned by the artist is, therefore in this case, one that allows him to throw the hoop forwards giving it, at the same time, spin in the opposite direction in order that the hoop returns to the hands of the owner. In this way, it almost seems as if the hoops were trained, and constantly throwing them all over the stage had a truly spectacular effect. These props were used for the first time in the circus ring in 1870 by an American clown named Globston.

It took another American, William Everhart, born in 1868, to make the most out of his great potential as a spectacular showpiece. The troupe of William Everhart performed mainly in America but around 1900 made a European tour where many artists saw them and where, thereafter, many imitators blossomed. The American Howard Nichols was in 1925 the first artists to develop truly difficult tossing combinations using hoops.

BOB BRAMSON

WILLIAM EVERHART TROUPE

BOB BRAMSON, HOOP ROLLING AND JUGGLING

In the world of entertainment, the name Bramson is synonymous with hoop rolling and juggling. In 1905, Berlin-born Paul Renner, who used the stage name Bramson, began to specialize in the hoopwork and was the first European act of its type. In 1910, he traveled with his first wife for four years in the United States. Paul Renner was the first artist to use hoops with electric lights. He actually took out German (in 1909), British, and American (in 1911) patents on this invention. In 1928 Paul Renner met his second wife, Gerti Rauch, in Moscow and trained her for his hoop act. While Everhart worked in Europe, Paul Renner (Bramson) performed as a duo in the United States. From 1933 on, Paul Renner worked with his wife Gerti as the 2 Bramsons. After 1943, they worked as a trio with their son Bob. Paul Renner suffered a heart attack on stage at the Apollo Theatre in Düsseldorf, Germany and he died in 1953.

Bob Bramson and his mother carried on the family act until 1964, then Bob began working solo. Bob Bramson's performance was full of original ideas that were unique among contemporary acts, as it demonstrated many difficult juggling moves with up to seven hoops. The hoop-rolling part of his routine also included some astounding moves. Bob Bramson also worked for two years with his wife in a second act as "Renner & Renner," using tennis rackets and flying Mexican sombreros. After a career spanning more than 50 years, Bob Bramson retired in 1999.

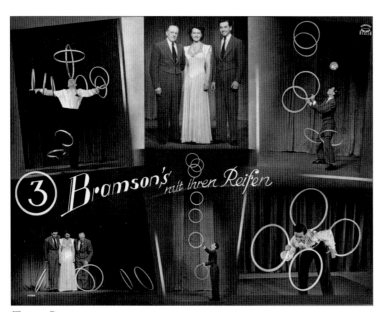

THE 3 BRAMSONS

FRANCIS BRUNN, IN A CLASS BY HIMSELF

FRANCIS BRUNN

Francis Brunn is without a doubt one of the most significant figures of the variety stage. The father of Francis was a German high-diving champion and Francis, who had a certain experience in this respect, was called to be a part of the training staff for high divers in the national Olympics. In 1938, Francis headed with his family to the Deutschlandhalle in Berlin to watch the circus show Menschen Tiere Sensationen (People, Animals, Sensations).[1] In 1939, Francis Brunn had with his sister Lottie his debut, and three years later he became the first person to juggle nine rings in performance.

In 1947, he broke his own record when he flashed 10 rings for the French newsreels in Paris. However, the insertion of such a record in his act lost him his gracefulness, which broke the internal cohesion that made up the greatest value of his act. Francis decided, therefore, to put the records aside and dedicate himself exclusively to the perfection of his movements. At the start of World War II, he was excused from service but notwithstanding, he was signed up by the most important circus of that time—the Ringling Bros. and Barnum & Bailey Circus in America. He was almost unable to honor his contract due to annoying bureaucratic problems, which forbade him from crossing the ocean. The much-wanted American entry visa only arrived in 1948. Once in America, Francis Brunn made a triumphant debut at Madison Square Garden in New York City, already a usual spring stop on the way to the great circus. The newspapers and magazines of that time named him: "Greater than Rastelli and 10 times faster."

Francis Brunn decided to leave the circus ring and go onto the variety stage. Lottie's part as Francis's assistant was taken over by Mary Tahmin, a New York actress. Instead of the silk costume he had worn until then, he now donned a close-fitting black bodysuit,

FRANCIS BRUNN

FRANCIS BRUNN

FRANCIS BRUNN

and incorporated Flemenco dance elements into his routine. He had always loved dance, and was particularly inspired by the famous Flemenco dancer Antonio Ruiz. During his eight minutes on stage, Francis Brunn did magical things with balls large and small, which came flying at him from the wings at ever-increasing speed. He caught not only with his hands, but on his head and the tips of his toes.

Francis was able to bounce a small tennis ball on his forehead, which he threw 9-12 feet into the air. He also spun a ball on his right index finger, which he held out in front of him, and with his left hand he threw a ball with an eclectic trajectory that made it end up on his shoulders. He then kicked the ball with his heel, sending it to land in front on the first ball where, reacting to the spinning ball, it started to also spin in the other direction.

Francis juggled with three rubber balls and passed a fourth from foot to foot at the same time he was jumping a rope spun by his assistant. His most celebrated feat, known as the Francis Brunn Routine, consisted of holding a stick between his teeth on which he spun a ball and another prop on his forehead. With his right leg he spun two rings, with his right arm another two rings, while he spun a balloon on his index finger. With his left hand he juggled with three rings. Above all, the exercises were carried out with a continuous flowing of captivating movements—fast and elegant and with delicate somersaults in the middle. Francis Brunn's assistant played a very important part in his act. Since 1980, this key role has been assumed by Nathalie Enterline. She performs by herself a solo dance routine in which she twirls and tosses a metal baton and Spanish hat. In May 2001, Francis Brunn directed and choreographed a Spanish Flemenco-tap dance show called Incognito, presented by the Tiger Palast Variety in Frankfurt, Germany.

BELA AND KRIS KREMO, THREE-OBJECT SPECIALISTS

Another important name in the history of juggling is that of Kremo. The family's tradition began around 1854 with a troupe, founded by Josef Kremo, specializing in Icarian Games. One of the youngest of the group, Karl, married a Hungarian girl called Margit Hannos. She had five children, amongst whom was Bela, born in 1911, who demonstrated himself to

LOTTIE BRUNN

KARL KREMO TROUPE, BELA KREMO SECOND FROM RIGHT

BELA KREMO

BELA AND KRIS KREMO

be an able juggler. While the main family attraction continued to be the Icarian Games, Bela sought to build a routine that would allow him to follow an individual path later on. Having been able to admire close-up a friend of his father's, Enrico Rastelli, this influenced his apprenticeship. Witnessing Rastelli's extremely vast and unsurpassable repertoire, Bela decided to abandon the hunt for the feat of the greatest number of objects, in unimaginable positions and complicated balances.

In this way, he began to dedicate himself to dazzling performances with just three objects, giving life to the first minimalist juggler being able, with discipline, tenacity and ambition, to reach exceptional heights.[2] He was the creator and master of the genre now called Three Piece and he chose as his props: gloves, balls, top hats, and cigar boxes, always only three in number. He debuted in 1931 at the Apollo in Aalborg as the second act of the family performance and, just three years later, took the solitary route that would eventually bring him international stardom. It is difficult to recount how the three cigar boxes moved agilely from one hand to another, remaining for just a few seconds suspended in the air, and how the top hats seemed to fight one another to stay in the privileged position of sitting on his head. Or how the three balls passed from right to left, up and down, with a devilish rhythm.

To compliment the harmony of his act, Bela performed all his tricks to the tempo of especially chosen music, while the entire performance was accompanied by a complex facial mimicry that underlined the various moments in his act. Bela wasn't really a comic juggler but his act had a strongly amusing component. His detachment from any stereotype of the jugglers then known brought him great and immediate success. After having performed in all the main halls of Europe, he was the first juggler to be hired on the luxurious stages of the great casinos of Las Vegas and, in the course of his long and fortunate career, he received a series of honors.

In 1970, he began performing with his 19-year-old son, Kris, in a double act that received much praise. In 1976, Bela Kremo retired, after almost 40 years of an honored career, and in 1976 he passed on to a better life with the knowledge of having left another Kremo to keep up the family name.

Kris (Kristian Gaston) Kremo was born in 1951 and

Yelena and Kris Kremo

performed in a double act with his father from 1970. His debut as a soloist happened in 1975, when he was hired for the summer season in one of the most elegant permanent circuses—the still-existing Blackpool Tower Circus. His success was immediate and the tam-tam of the other workers made it immediately understood that another star was born. To confirm these rosy forecasts he was quickly called to take part in the Royal Command Variety Performance, the annual gala show at London's Palladium for the Royal Family, who had witnessed the presence of Paul Cinquevalli more than half a century before.

Kris continues even today to be hired by the most important venues in the world. More than carrying on his father's tradition, he has been able to include in his act some exploits that have been worthy of Guinness World Records. Among these were the triple pirouette, incredible for the speed at which it was executed, carried out after throwing a cigar box that he caught at the end of his turn. In 1977, Kris Kremo even surpassed his own brilliant best by becoming the first artist to complete a quadruple pirouette with cigar boxes.

Kris Kremo is married to the Russian artist Yelena Alexy Larkina, known for her hula-hoop number called Fata Morgana, choreographed by Valentin Gneouchev. After touring in 1991 with the Swiss Circus Knie, Kris Kremo realized a long-treasured dream: a solo program of his own. The juggling-fantasy story Catch, scripted by Kremo himself and featuring Kris and a cast of 12, opened at the theatre in Connyland theme park in Lipperswil, Switzerland. In March 2002, he and his wife Yelena performed a one-hour show together with the Basel Symphonic Orchestra.

The first juggler to perform single pirouettes with cigar boxes was the Englishman Peter Woodrow in 1950, followed 10 years later by the German artist Rudy Schweitzer.

ANTHONY GATTO, JUGGLING RECORD-HOLDER

If one has to nominate a juggler who resides in these circuits the choice without hesitation is the phenomenon Anthony Gatto, considered to be the juggler with the greatest technical ability of our day. Anthony was born in 1973 in Ellicot City, Maryland. He began training at a very young age and because of his ability and youth, at the age of seven he appeared in the highly viewed American television show *That's Incredible.* In 1983, at nine years of age, he won the Gold Medal at the Festival du Demain in Paris. That same year he won a minor prize at the Festival de Monte Carlo, where nonetheless, he was later destined to triumph.

In 1986 the magazine *Sports Illustrated* commissioned a long article about him and here is an excerpt: "A 13-year-old American can hold balls, clubs, and rings in the air longer that any other juggler alive today." From then on, he had an unending series of participations at juggling conventions, television programs, festivals, and circus and juggler meetings. However, his main engagements were in the grand venues of Las Vegas, where he was continually in demand, leaving him very little time for foreign visits.

BOBBY MAY AND ANTHONY GATTO, OHIO 1981

In 1989, his name is quoted in the *Guinness Book of Records* under four different categories: Seven and eight clubs, seven-lit torches, and the five-club endurance without dropping (45 minutes and two seconds). On June 22, 1993, before an audience of invited guests, journalists and photographers in Berlin's Wintergarten variety theatre, Anthony Gatto became the first artist to flash 12 rings in public. Suddenly in 1995, at just 22 years of age, when contending for the title of the world's greatest juggler, Anthony decided to retire. He opened a gardening firm and dedicated himself entirely to this.

In February 1998, after two-and-a-half years of total inactivity, he decided to return to his art and in nine weeks he took his act back to the same high standard as before. Nearly two years after his return, in January 2000, Anthony took part in the XXIV International Circus Festival in Monte Carlo. He complained about the organization, which didn't allow him even 15-minutes of practice in the ring. He was forced to train for merely a few minutes before the public opening, in a corner between the animal cages and the red-velvet curtain.

His preparations were astonishing: eight clubs; six clubs with a forehead balance; seven clubs bouncing a ball on his forehead; nine balls; and 10, 11, then 12 rings. His father Nick, holding a stop-watch in his hand, said to Anthony: "Make a good throw with 10, hold it a little longer, bring back your left arm a little."

It was finally time for the performance in front of the jury, which also included Prince Ranier of Monaco. Anthony presented himself in a simple and elegant way—with a sincere smile, even while he carried out his most difficult feats. Beyond the seven clubs and 11 rings, he amazed the audience with his "five-and-seven" ring routine with a full pirouette, with four clubs and a ball, and for the ease with which he juggled five clubs in all the possible ways: in front, behind the back one arm at a time, behind the back with both arms, above the head, even under the legs (Alberts). Anthony is one of the few jugglers at the moment to combine pure juggling with balancing. For example, when he held a three-foot-long pole on his forehead, on which there were cups attached, he juggled five balls that, one after another, finished up in the cups.

A triumph for Anthony. A standing ovation at the gala evening and a Gold Clown Award—the first time it has been awarded to a juggler.

ANTHONY GATTO

Before him there had only been five silver awards, given to Dick Franco, Kris Kremo, Sergei Ignatov, Picaso Junior, and Viktor Kee. It is important to remember the fundamental contribution to Nick, who in his youth was part of the acrobatic trio, Los Gattos Trios. Nick worked in the best venues of Las Vegas but was destined to be thereafter remembered as the coach of the world's greatest juggler.

---

1 *Mensche, Tiere und Sensationen*
2 K.H. Ziethen, 1988, op. cit.

ANTHONY GATTO

ANTHONY GATTO

ANTHONY AND NICK GATTO

VII

JUGGLING IN RUSSIA AND CHINA

THE MOSCOW SCHOOL OF CIRCUS,
BEGINNING OF A METHODICAL APPROACH

In the history of Russian circus, the Italian artists have had a noteworthy importance. Alessandro Guerra, "The Furious," was the first Italian to establish himself in Russia, constructing in 1845 a wooden building that he, a little presumptuously, called the Cirque Olimpique. However, the most important Italian directors to work in the Russian territory were the Cinisellis. They were entrepreneurs who were very aware of the novelty of that era, as attested by the inclusion of projections of the first films and performances of high-level dancers into their programs, amongst which was the great French dancer, Cleo de Merode—the mother of Nijinskij.

Other famous directors were the Truzzis, much appreciated pantomime scenographers and owners of traveling circuses. The presence of these Italian directors at that time was held in great regard, stimulating without doubt the arrival of a multitude of artists into that country who were hopeful to win over the solidarity of their more fortunate fellow countrymen.[1] At that time, the pantomimes were much appreciated. This demanded a healthy number of artists, for work which, however insignificant or badly paid, was never lacking. In this way, Russia became a second home for the Italian circus artists.

According to Jewgeni Kusnezow, the founder of Russian circus historiography, the composition of the Russian cities was rather complicated. The workers of the

ALBERT PETROVSKI

very famous Putilov Laboratory, for example, often headed to watch the best-loved shows of that time rather than visit other buildings frequented by aristocrats. In St. Petersburg, the Modern Zirkus specifically opened for those who were not so well off; while the rich continued to crowd the Ciniselli, which was considered more careful in the choice and quality of the performances and the elegance of the surroundings. The members of the important families even went to the extent of holding extremely expensive performances in the privacy of their own homes.

This well-being only lasted up to the start of World War I, which brought serious changes to the Russian circus arts.[2] Many artists were signed up for army duty and would never return home again. Money was short and the public deserted all forms of spectacles. Only at the end of the war was there a minor revival that brought the creation of new permanent circuses, traveling circuses and variety theatres. Already from 1914 an association of class was founded in Moscow and, during the great war paradoxically, many central European artists preferred to stay in the great Russian nation, where they felt safer than in their far-away countries upset by military activity.

After the start of war in 1914 (considered by Lenin to be the "accelerator of history") and after three years of difficult government up to 1917, the most important revolution in our time happened. In February there was the revolution of the upper-classes and by October there was that of the working-classes. On August 26, 1919, Lenin, following the proposal by the Education Secretary and that of the Cultural Secretary, Anatlij Vasileviic Lunaciarsky, published a decree for the nationalization of the theatres and circuses, entrusting the coordination of all permanent and traveling circuses existing in the Russian territory. Furthermore, all workers in the sector were encompassed in a single directive organ—the Soyuzgoscyrk—whose first responsibility was the Austrian juggler, Darlë.

In 1927, the Moscow School of Circus and Variety Arts opened, where learning juggling was obligatory and taught from the very start of courses. Briefly, the arts of the circus blossomed in all aspects. The 15 national circuses became 86 and the figure of Circus Director was born, who, through a close collaboration of artists, choreographers, and composers, allowed the creation of true circus works of art. The school was combined, in 1946,

ALEXANDER AND VIOLETTA KISS

with the study of the formation and preparation of artists, acts, and circus programs—a laboratory of avant-garde circus arts where they experimented with new possible techniques and creativity in every discipline.

However, the most important innovation regarding the development of juggling was the birth of true and modern teaching methods. Representative of this was the case of one of the greatest figures of the pedagogy of such a discipline, Violetta Kiss, who passed from the role of a great artist to that of an esteemed professor. The most famous duet of juggling acrobats from the era before World War II was that of the "Kiss Children." Alexander, born in 1921, and Violetta, born in 1925, came from a circus family and their mother was of Italian origin.

Their mother was, in fact, the daughter of Alessandro Ciniselli, who did a lot to spread the circus in Russia. Their father, on the other hand, was Nikolai Kiss and together with another talented Russian artist, Boris Borisow, created a famous juggling horseback act, The Borkiss, in which Alexander made his debut at 12 years of age. That act, created at the end of the 1930's, depicted a group of holidaymakers engaged in a merry picnic in which the eight members of the group threw bottles, plates, apples, and anything else that was available. This was practically another variation

ALEXANDER KISS

of the famous restaurant act (which also included feats with horses), because it needed an open-air setting, hence the picnic scene.

The artists were precariously balanced upon a horse-drawn cart, or even on the back of the horse, and they carried out crossing passes with the other artists while galloping on other horses or standing down in the center of the ring. For the finale, the lights were dimmed and they performed with lighted torches instead of clubs. The two Kiss brothers were among the first artists to make use of complete State assistance, with planned training and performances in specially adapted places. The props were expressly designed and constructed from the latest technological products. Their debut was in 1939, when Alexander and Violetta presented an act that demonstrated the skill they had acquired in the various forms of juggling, antipodism and balancing.

Even this new creation had a particular setting, which was that of a child's playroom, where a small quarrel blew up between the two. This was only a pretext to start a series of incredible feats. Alexander and Violetta Kiss performed the freestanding ladder, rola-bola, hand-to-hand and hand-to-head exploits. During the course of their long career they invented more than 40 new feats. The best known was that in which Alexander balanced on a rola-bola, with a cane and ball balanced on his forehead, while juggling up to eight rings. He invented new harmonies with the clubs, which were only possible through rigorous technical and ballistic studies. When the duet dissolved in 1966, Violetta taught in the circus school, while Alexander and his children became ringmasters. Violetta soon demonstrated to be as able a teacher as an artist.

The Kiss School was born, to become known as "the method" where a tutor passes on all his acquired knowledge. Even with juggling, Russia confirmed itself as the maestro of the methodical approach, as had already happened for the more important recital arts. The Moscow School of Circus and Variety Arts produced about ten good jugglers and a significant number of talented instructors. Nikolai Ernestowitsch Baumann was signed on at the school from the very beginning. He graduated in 1930 and, together with his companion, W. Metjolkin, created an acrobatic juggling act of a high level. While Baumann juggled with three clubs, the other person, behind him, threw him another two, which he caught and thereby inserted into the maneuver. After six years of practice, they inserted into their act the double-balance on their forehead, in which one balanced head-down on top of the head of the other, each person juggling three clubs. They then passed them to one another without changing their positions.

In 1947, Nikolai Ernestowitsch Baumann became a professor at the same school from which he had graduated 17 years earlier. He holds an important first—he was the first tutor to write and publish a juggling manual to use in his classes, hence creating the Baumann Method, which was the sum of all the teachings he had received from the institute and from his personal experiences in many years of activity.3 Both the teachings of Baumann and that of Violetta adopted the same innovative techniques that were originally introduced by Enrico Rastelli, creating the logical follow up.

One of the first graduates of the Moscow School of Circus and Variety Arts was juggler Albert Machlin, who developed many original tricks, using the mouth-stick and a ball. The

YEWGENI BILJAUER

FOUR PROKOFIES

brothers Ivan and Yewgeni Chromow demonstrated the classical Rastelli techniques, and Konstantin Nikolskij bounced three balls on his forehead. One of the first Russian jugglers to become a top-class circus performer was Albert Petrovski. He was able to juggle eight or 10 rings while bouncing a ball on his head. A model for the new generation of Russian jugglers in the 1960's was Eduard Abert, who came from a famous circus family. He juggled in his parent's troupe, the 5 Aberts, and performed solo with up to five clubs and 10 rings. Yewgeni Biljauer was able to perform feats of the highest degree of difficulty, becoming the first artist to juggle six clubs while bouncing a ball on his forehead, or to pirouette during a five-club juggle.

An outstanding female juggler was Nasi Shirai. She performed in an Armenian folk costume and juggled five batons, seven balls, and eight rings, and she even used up to six tambourines as juggling props. Maja Rubtsova balanced a perch on her forehead, on top of which sat a teddy bear. She juggled with seven rings and finally tossed them into the paws of the stuffed toy.

In the 1970's, classical juggling with balls, clubs and rings reached a pinnacle in the shape of Sergei Ignatov, born in 1950. At age 16, he made his entrance into the Moscow School of Circus and Variety Arts, where Violetta Kiss immediately noted his particular talent and wanted to have him in the course. In part due to the teachings of Violetta, and in part due to his innate artistic talents, Sergei soon became a juggling phenomenon. He

THREE GRATSCHEWIS

was able to break new world records, in as much as the number of objects he could juggle, and was able to express his technique in a harmonic fusion with millisecond precision to the timing of the music and the rhythm of the objects thrown. A beautiful feat to watch was the pirouette performed with seven rings suspended in the air while he turned around.

Before anything else, he was considered a juggling poet. He had created passes with three, four and five clubs that were both spectacular and distinguished, which he performed to the piano music of Chopin. Sergei was able to juggle with five and even seven large balls, almost the size of coconuts and up to nine when practicing. For his five-club routine, Ignatov used an interesting method for picking up clubs with his feet. While juggling four clubs, he stamp on the end of the fifth, that was lying on the floor, so that it turned a somersault in mid-air and dropped into his right hand, only to be seamlessly integrated into what was now a five-club juggle. He also created a new variation with rings. In the middle of his juggle, he turned his palms upwards and outwards so that the rings started spinning around a horizontal axis, like pancakes being tossed from a frying pan. Sergei Ignatov is a superlative juggler of nine rings and he has managed up to 135 consecutive throws. In 1973, in the United States, he raised juggling onto a new plane when he succeeded in flashing 11 rings, starting with nine and then detaching another two from a special belt.

Other juggling talents to come out of the school in Moscow were the Kisses, compatriots Yuro and Sinaida Birjukowy and the 4 Prokofies, all of whom have demonstrated outstanding club and ring passing while staying on the head. A special technical achievement was made by the 2 Laclaschwili's, who juggled on two rotating slack-ropes. Sigmund Tschernjauskas has also proved his outstanding skills. With his partner, Vita, he mastered the most-difficult balance-juggling tricks not only on the free-standing ladder, but also on the high unicycle. Gregory Popowitch is currently the world's foremost juggler with clubs and rings on the free-standing ladder. When not on the ladder, he juggles up to nine balls in practice.

Nikolai Gerassimov attended the Moscow School of Circus and Variety Arts in 1996. He has discovered a new way to throw clubs and rings: sideways ("flat-throws" with the long axis rotating parallel to the body). The first Russian performer who juggled with 10 balls was Alexander Bresizkin in 1970. He did not work in the circus, but in stage shows called Estrade. Many famous Russian Estrade jugglers have never performed in the western world, but one who did was Michael Rudenko from the Ukraine, who worked with up to five spinning balls. Rudenko was the first juggler to use small sand-filled balls, kicking them up from the floor with his feet. Timour Kaibjanov, from Moscow, is the first juggler to juggle three balls entirely with his feet (completely unaided by his hands). He performs this while sitting on a bar stool.

The first club-passing troupes were the Krenkos and the Koshuchows, and in 1951 the Moscow school brought out an original act Jugglers on the Pole, under the direction of N.E Baumann and performed by the Three Gratschewis. It was a very spectacular creation for the new and multiple combinations of juggling and acrobatics that were being presented. In the ring, there were two fixed poles anchored to the ground, about six feet high. Half way up each pole there was a robust harness that allowed the artists to insert a foot, with the other foot pushing against the pole, in the position of a flag. In this way the two jugglers remained as though suspended on the poles and in this unusual position they passed clubs and rings, even from behind their backs. Between the poles there was a slack rope suspended on which a third artist walked who, in his own turn, juggled with the other two performers.

A new generation of club-passers who began performing in the mid-'70s came in the form of the troupe Gibadulin's. Damir Gibadulin, from Kazan in the Tatar Republik, along

SERGEI IGNATOV WITH HIS DAUGHTER KATJA

with his wife Margarita, built a six-person troupe when they left the Moscow school in 1969. The troupe developed innovative club-passing patterns with acrobatic tricks and dance moves, including a feat in which one standing partner passes clubs to partners who are lying down. Damir Gibadulin also produced the unique trick of passing 16 clubs between four people at a distance of 40 feet. The Gibadulins were the first troupe who performed passing figures without stopping, in complete darkness with phosphorescent clubs. Morat Shageevm, who has performed now for 32 years in the Gibadulin troupe, is the only person who can throw out of his hand, four, five and six plates at once to his partners standing in front of him.

In the meantime, owing to the powerful organization Soyuzgoscryk, which put engineers and thinkers at their disposal, even in juggling, new and original acts were created in which the skill of the artists was emphasized in favor of the technical wizards. In 1973, the Garssenwanischwili Trio (five years later known as the Four Afanasjewis) came out of the school, a trio that used a complicated mechanical apparatus with two crane arms which, thanks to a hydraulic system, could reach the height of four meters from the ground and spin around the ring. On the summit of the arms, two small platforms were positioned on which sat the artists. From up there, they threw clubs from one part of the ring to another. A third member of the group juggled in the center of the equipment.

Anatoli Tchjan and Viktor Rakin was the first duo to pass 10 clubs in 1972. Also, the Two Miagkostoupovs (Anatoli Miagkostoupov and Viktor Pilipovich) were very strong technical club jugglers both individually and as a team. They graduated in the mid-1980's from the Circus School in Kiev (Ukraine). Their teachers were Alexander Grusin and Alisa Aslanian. The Two Miagkostoupovs juggled clubs in disco-dance style, with acrobatic elements. A previously unseen trick was their five-club routine, in which the clubs were exchanged sideways, backwards, or under the legs from one partner to the other without interrupting the patterns.

GIBADULINS

Since 1991, Anatoli Miagkostoupov has been performing with his wife Ivena a cube act which combines ballet and jazz movements, balancing, tumbling and aerial acrobatic feats.

The Soviet Model was implanted in practically all the countries in the Socialist Block of that time: Poland, Hungary, East Germany, even Cuba and North Korea, and they all had their circus schools where jugglers graduated very well prepared.

After the recent changes, and the fall of the Soviet Union, the panorama of the jugglers also changed. The Soyuzgoscyrk has become Rosgoscyrk (no longer the Soviet Union but now Russia) and the enormous Soviet artistic and personnel wealth had been reduced to only 6000 artists. The capitals that were previously considered "out of the empire," such as Minsk, Kiev, and Riga, have now developed their own plans, which often bear unexpected fruit even in juggling.

In Moscow, a new circus era started in the mid-1980's with the choreographer Valentin Gneoucher, who brought out several juggling acts such as Vladimir Tsarkov, Evgeni Pimonenko, Andrei Ivachnenko, the Duo Bondarenko, Ruslan Fomenko, Dimitri Abert. Top-level newcomers to juggling in the new millenium include Lajos Nereus (Hungary), Youri Borzykine (Ukraine), Mario Berousek (Czech Republic), Claudius

TWO MIAGKOSTOUPOVS

Specht (Swizterland), and Oliver Groszer (Germany). Add to this list, Yeton, who followed the steps of gentleman juggler Felix Adanos, Tuan Le, from Vietnam, and Paul Ponce, from Argentina, who learned his juggling from his father, Victor Ponce.

THE NEW CHINA

In the century just ended, China has lived through numerous changes that have influenced in a decisive way the means of presenting and enjoying the activity of folk-performances. At the start of the twentieth century in China, the jugglers weren't able to obtain a decent lifestyle and for this reason many emigrated abroad. However, in 1949,

YIAN PING QIAN

with the birth of the new China and the advent of Mao Tse-Tung, the nationalization of the acrobatic companies was effectuated and this allowed for note-worthy development.

It was remarkably the Prime Minister Zhou Enlai who ordered the first acrobatic display for the new China in October of 1950 in Peking at the Huairen Hall of Zhongnanhai. It involved a group formed by acrobats, from the entire nation, chosen personally by Enlai, who had written: "Acrobatics should give an aesthetic pleasure and a pleasant sensation to the people." The freak shows were eliminated, also the excessiveness of the fakirs, and also those acts based upon "brutal" sensations. Hazardous components were also limited and rigorous safety measures were introduced. The success of performances of the first acrobatic company—the New China Acrobatic Troupe—was such as to inspire the birth of many similar groups throughout the entire Chinese territory.

In China, there are actually over 100 acrobatic companies, not coordinated, but all under the responsibility of the Culture Minister. All the companies perform on stages, except in the rare cases where a big top is used, apparently influenced by western customs. Only more recently have richer, permanent circuses been built. The company, the central nucleus of the acrobatic activity in China, is formed by a minimum of 40 people and up to a maximum of 150. Usually, it is divided into two distinct sections—that of work and that of preparation.

In the working sector, the more mature artists are organized and directed into groups that must firstly please the local people, and then, if the necessary requirements are met, the artists may carry out a tour inside the national territory or even abroad. In the preparatory group, very young pupils are taught the various acrobatic disciplines. Here the need is felt to collaborate closely with choreographers and directors, and furthermore with dressmakers, designers and scenographers, with the aim of making the very highest level of artistry out of street acrobatics. Owing to the mixing with other cultural forms, acrobatics in China has become a composite and harmonious art form, with frequent references to myths and popular legends or themes, many often performed at the Opera of Peking.

From an anthropological point of view, it is interesting to note what has happened at Wuquiao, Liaocheng, Yancheng and Tiananmen, places that enjoy the title of "House of Acrobatics." In these places, all the inhabitants perform acrobatic feats in the street and also juggle, just as playing football or hide-and-seek is a social recreation for us.

At the end of 1981, the first Chinese acrobatics convention was held in which more than 170 delegates participated from all over the country. During the meeting, the Acrobatic Arts Association was founded and with this the Acrobatics and Magic magazine was first published, dedicated to every aspect of the acrobatic and illusionist arts. According to some Chinese statisticians, there are more than 12,000 artists engaged in a variety of incredible disciplines in over 200 different categories. This was helped by the fact that the single components of every company were taught to perform more routines, with a particular attention to that in the group. That ended up as a disadvantage for the jugglers, who needed a more specific and intensive training.

For this reason juggling isn't one of the most widespread disciplines in the great nation. More practiced is antipodism, the spinning meteors and cup throwing while on a unicycle, not to mention the art of balancing objects and shuttlecock kicking (which is completely unheard of in Europe). The return of the tradition of the diabolo carried out

CHINESE JAR JUGGLERS AT CIRCUS ALEXIS GRUSS

Fu Xiu Yu

by the acrobatic companies near Shanghai has allowed Tian Shuangliang to come to light—an artist who uses a particular diabolo not made of wood but of bronze, helped by four youths who made up delicate evolutions surrounded by a dark-red scenery between which the ancient Chinese toy acquired a semblance of a green moon. Another talented artist was Fan Xue Ping, able to juggle eight balls on a rola-bola.

However, it was the Qian Brothers from the acrobatic company of Nanjing, who affirmed the Chinese juggling. Jian Ping, Jian Hua and Jian Wen Qian descended from an ancient dynasty of jugglers and their grandfather, Bingzahang, was a well-noted acrobat. Jian Ping has an unfaltering command of three-to-seven badminton racquets, can juggle five with solid backcrosses for one minute, and has performed a flash with eight racquets. The youngest brother, Jian Hua, is the baseman for the acrobatic balancing. In their finale, they stand in a line formation, each juggling six rings, then break into an 18-ring passing pattern.

Fu Xiu Yu performs a hitherto unequaled combination in which she tosses bowls onto her head—as many as five at once—while riding a high unicycle atop a rolling globe. Because of the strong tradition for foot-juggling, Chinese artists have attained an outstanding degree of excellence in this genre.

1 Kusnezow, Yewgeni, Zirk, 1938, *Der Zirkus der Welt*, Berlin, Henschelverlag Kunst und Geselschaft, 1970, p. 192.

2 We mustn't forget that Kusnezow wrote his important study in 1938 in the midst of the Soviet regime.

3 Baumann, Nikolai Ernestowitsch, *Die Kunst des Jonglierens*, Leipzig, Germany, Zentralhaus fur Kulturarbeit der DDR, 1962, p. 148.

VIII

CONTEMPORARY JUGGLERS

NEW MARKETS

Exploring the past, we have dwelt upon a few example artists and have read their careers as if they represented the various phases of the entire category. This type of analysis is much more difficult today, mainly due to the enormous spread and evolution that juggling has known in the last few decades of the 20th century. This chapter identifies three principal places for the performance of contemporary juggling: the traditional market (circuses, plays, variety theatres, etc.); the street (conventions, buskers, festivals, street theatre); and the new circuits (theatrical seasons, festivals, and individual performances). For each of these places we propose a brief description and name a juggler who is noteworthy in that field.

THE STREET AND INNOVATION

Some time ago, in 1947, a group of passionate young American jugglers decided to create the International Jugglers Association (IJA), an association for the lovers of the juggling art, both amateurs and professionals. The objectives of the IJA, with more than 3,000 members, has always been to ease the exchange between jugglers and to allow the art to broaden among the profane. The IJA can boast numerous contacts with similar associations throughout the world. In 1978, the European Juggling Convention (EJC) convened in Europe, in which thousands of jugglers from

FREDERICK "BOULE" ZIPPERLIN

LA SALLE BROTHERS

the whole of Europe participated. This event, which has become an annual affair, inspired the birth of national conventions on the whole continent.

At the same time, taking inspiration from something different than the traditional and previously known artists, a new American trend of Fantasy Jugglers started with jugglers who returned to the street and open air to find a new freshness and spontaneity in their contact with the audience. The movement of the Fantasy Jugglers can be illustrated with some of the players, for example: the Flying Karamazov Brothers, the Bay City Reds, Passing Fancy, Wimbledon Brothers, Airjazz, the duos Raspyni Brothers, Passing Zone, Doubble Troubble and La Salle Brothers, plus Ray Jason, Edward Jackman, and Steve Mills. The jugglers, comedians, mimes, magicians, and musicians were all part of the countercultural movement of the time.

The ropewalker, unicyclist, magician, juggler and pantomime performer Philippe Petit was the earliest modern-day street juggler in Paris in 1968. On August 7, 1974, he walked a tight-rope between the twin towers at the 110th floor of the World Trade Center. At the Covent Garden, London, he performed in Britain's most-successful duo of the mid-1980's, Mr. Adams and Mr. Dandridge, as well as with Sean Gandini. The mid-1980's saw also a new generation of jugglers, like Oliver Groszer and Markus Jeroch in Germany. For them, street performing proved to be the right venue for starting out. In 1988, when more and more theatres specialized in physical entertainment, these artists became regulars on the stages of Germany's new variety theatres.

It is also in gratitude to this incredible movement that, at the start of the 1980's, one can see the emergence of a new generation of jugglers for which the aesthetic criteria is more important than the technical mastery. At the American IJA convention in 1967, a 13-year-old Michael Moschen took part in what would later revolutionize the art of juggling. Moschen, one of four brothers from a simple family whose father worked in a factory, was born in 1954, in Greenfield, Massachusetts. His first scholarly results were somewhat deceiving since in his words, "In life you must educate yourself rather than learning things from others." In this way he left his studies to become a potter. The handcraft aspect to his character is as dominant as his dexterity, both of which he gained from his grandfather, a sculpture of Italian origins.

At 12 years of age, Michael began juggling with his brother Colin and his neighbor Penn Jillette (destined to become famous in the United States as a comic magician in the duet Penn and Teller). Together they watched a television special on Francis Brunn and were very impressed. In 1967, Michael went to his first juggling convention and he immediately started to meet and learn from numerous people. He didn't confine himself though to just juggling. At 18, he attended a course in stretching with the Massachusetts University gymnastics team. He then went on to take lessons in ballet, tap, jazz, martial arts, tai chi and acrobatics.

During this period, he began work with Peter Cunneen, using club- swinging techniques that he developed into his own original fire dance. He started working in the streets of New York City, choosing a piece of pavement in front of the Metropolitan Museum of Modern Art. Michael soon distinguished himself when the Big Apple Circus, which had just been founded by Paul Binder and Michael Christensen, hired him in 1977. He worked for three years with the Big Apple Circus and experimented a great deal. His act lasted eight minutes, during which he used two greatly different styles: a light, comical three-ball routine and a fire-swinging act that emphasized his technique.

Some of Michael's skills with the fire torches were used in the film *Hair,* directed by Milos Forman (1979). He worked with Lotte Goslar's Pantomime Circus. He became known in the dance and show circuits. In the 70's, he had become the pioneer of the genre of contact, which meant, instead of throwing and catching objects, the objects are run around the limbs and follow extremely refined body movements and the harmony of the objects. Michael describes this type of performance as manipulation.

Michael then decided to work with crystal balls, one of his most famous creations. At the start he didn't know what to do with them, so he typically carried out simple figures, which then grew, leaving the ball to transmit something. For instance, he decided to never close his hand around the ball. He eventually learned to turn around more than one sphere (to ultimately become eight in two hands). He would say, "the crystal

MICHAEL MOSCHEN

MICHAEL MOSCHEN

balls represented a way of relating ourselves with the fragility of the world." The use of natural elements, such as fire or completely transparent balls, gives in some way a metaphysical connotation to Michael's act.

He played the hands of David Bowie, who juggles with crystal balls in the film *Labyrinth* (1986). After the crystal balls, came the sticks—and he even used these in a highly innovative way. In the 1980's, Michael performed with Fred Garbo and Bob Berky in the group Foolsfire. He collaborated in the play *The Alchemists* off-Broadway in 1986. In 1988, he created a true one-man show: Michael Moschen in Motion, which he took to numerous theatres and dance festivals in Hong Kong, Perth, Edinburgh, Barcelona, and Spoleto. It was during that period that he created another of his famous inventions: the man-sized wooden triangle, inside which he would bounce up to five silicone balls, playing with the musical rhythm that he created by juggling with the hands, feet, and head, so fast that the balls appeared to leave trails.

In the 90's, he became responsible for juggling in Cirque du Soleil and he dedicated himself to the invention of new techniques and new props. He has had numerous appearances in successful television programs, too. In 1991, he created and directed the special *In Motion with Michael Moschen* for the series *Great Performances* produced by the PBS.

For Michael, juggling means "investing your spirit in something that you don't know the outcome of and what may very well fail."

THE "NEW ERA"

Another important phenomenon for the development of juggling has been the birth of Nouveau Cirque. The motivations for such a movement are to be found in the activities that around 1968 contributed a little everywhere in the development of new theatre which looked to break the old schemes and take their own energy to more authentic performance forms, such as the commedia dell'arte and mime (that were very similar to the circus).[1] Elsewhere, there was a profound and profitable blending of styles that gave way to experiences such as Pina Bausch's theatre-dance, plus the activity of Arianne Mnouchkine, or even the Bread and Puppet Theatre.

In the early 1970's, the circus offered a somewhat static artistic form. The fusion between elements of circus and theatre created a reciprocal, positive influence, determining interesting innovations. Let's remember the revolutionary performances of Jerome Savary and his Grand Magic Circus or that of the refined poetry of Victoria Chaplin and Jean Baptist Thierrè with their Cirque Imaginaire.

A further stimulus to juggling's development came from the birth of western schools— inspired by those from the ex-socialist Eastern Block. In 1985, with the backing of Jack Lang, the French Culture Minister at that time, France built its first public circus school to be recognized by the government. The Centre National des Arts du Cirque (CNAC), which resides at Châlons-sur-Marne (France), is gifted with a vast multimedia archive detailing the circus culture. The school at Châlons has been an example for many other countries and there has been a blossoming of circus schools throughout Europe, among which we shall cite at least the Circus Space in London, Carampa in Madrid, and Líecole in Brussels. Across the ocean, the Ecole

VIKTOR KEE

MICHAEL MOSCHEN

du Cirque de Montreal has become very important—making research and innovation its strong point.

However, the spirit of the new circus has traveled the world thanks to the success of the Canadian group, Cirque du Soleil. "If you haven't got a voice, shout! If you haven't got legs, run! If you haven't any hope, invent!" This is the slogan of *Alegria*, one of the latest productions of Soleil, which, as a whole has revolutionized the way of making circus, both from the point of view of the aesthetic approach and that of their marketing and sales techniques. The slogan doesn't reflect at all the requirements of the creative staff of the Cross Atlantic Colossal, in as much as in voice, legs and hope they don't need to envy anyone!

Cirque du Soleil has four main bases: an international office in Montreal; a second office in Amsterdam (which handles European activity); an office in Las Vegas; and a new office in Singapore. Soleil's approach to the global concept of performance has also been a stimulus for the renovation of the singular specialty in the ring. The visionaries of Soleil, surrounded by experts in various disciplines, have brought substantial changes in the antique typologies, such as trapeze, acrobatics on the ground and on the elastic trampoline and, obviously, juggling.

Other than hosting jugglers gifted with a notable technique in their shows—such as the Cuban Miguel Herrera, the Mexican Octavio Alegria, the Dutchman Eric Borgmann, the Ukrainian Viktor Kee, the Russian Maria Choodu, and the Israeli Sergei Dydk—the creators of Soleil looked to revitalize the discipline by working on character and inventing new techniques. The first most significant example is that of the Frenchman Frederick Zipperlin, who gave life to the character of "Boule," a baby-bird buffoon juggler. Boule is a strange creature that comes out of the water. His character was created in 1989, the time when his mask was thought up, which Zipperlin was able to give identity to—not just a buffoon born from a large bubble but also a great juggler. Boule lives in a spherical world: he comes from a large bubble and feeds and juggles with objects the size and shape of ping-pong balls.

With regard to the invention of new props and techniques, Soleil entrusted Michael Moschen, who from the mid-1990's has become the man in charge of juggling at Cirque du Soleil, especially dedicated to the inventions of new things, such as the metal sheets used for juggling white balls.

JUGGLING IN THEATRES

Thanks especially to Michael Moschen's activity, juggling has assumed a creative and financial autonomy with regards to the circus and variety, a phenomenon also known as the democratization of circus disciplines. The various specialties leave the ring to assume their own life, as has happened in the past with clowns, acrobats, equestrians and aerial performers. While, for the whole of the 1800's and 1900's, the of juggler's performances consisted of acts of pure technique—often not lasting for more than 10 minutes. They are now becoming true and proper artistic creations with a duration of even an hour, which allows these avant-garde jugglers to explore the most diverse theatrical presentations, to create their own recital and to perform them on the most important stages in the world.

One of the chief examples of the new interpretation of juggling is Jerome Thomas. His choice to become a juggler goes back more than 20 years ago, when the traveling company Compagnie Foraine visited his home city. That vision instilled in the young man, barely 14, the passion for the art and stimulated him to go to Annie Fratellini's Circus School in Paris. Jerome learned a solid technical base in the discipline, winning a Bronze medal in the Louis Martin Trophy (at the Festival du Cirque de Demain). He immediately found work performing in French circuses and cabaret, presenting an act with the classic circus structure. Soon after, he decided to orientate himself towards a different style of juggling, a sort of "juggling jazz" and he collaborated with many musicians.

Jerome's style of creation was principally based on three criteria: the double bounce; the union of "heaven and earth" and the choice of a single object; and the white silicone ball. The fact that the ball bounces twice makes the ball run away from the artist for an instant and seems to have a life of its own. The choice of juggling both up and down allows a large range of movements. Lastly, the choice of a unique object gives his performance a particular characteristic—the neutrality of the object allows it to assume its own personality, obviously through Jerome's skillful manipulation. In this way, each ball,

JÉROME THOMAS AND PHILIPPE MÉNARD

depending on the movements that they are made to make and the posture of the juggler seem to assume their own character. There is, therefore, an aggressive ball that frightens the artist, an inebriated ball that is uncontrollable, even a ball that is in love, which follows him everywhere.

This is another of Jerome's innovations that allow him, moreover, to build a one-man show, which is always different and rich in stimulus and in which the audience ends up not identifying themselves with the actor but with the balls instead, following the various and often-opposing destinies. One can read his breakaway from the preceding traditions in three ways: aesthetic, ethical and technical.

Aesthetic because Jerome's juggling is theatrical, poetical, improvisatory and gives way to a new genre, that of the juggled theatre which comes close to the standards of modern dance with performances lasting up to 90 minutes each, at the same time acquiring an autonomy regarding the circus. From the ethical point of view, Jerome distinguishes himself for his choice of leaving the purely commercial circus and variety circuits and, later on, for the will to substitute the solitude of a creative genius for that of group work. From a technical point of view, for the construction of an alphabet of the classical base figures of juggling, which allows the composition of precise choreographic scores at the same time, there is ample space for Jerome to improvise—a practice also acquired due to the fact that he attended jazz music sessions.

JÉROME THOMAS

AirJazz

Jerome created spectacular shows, among which we remember Artrio, Extraball, and Kulbuto. He founded ARMO (Association of Research in Object Manipulation). He furthermore created Quipos, Hic Hoc, Le Banquet, and Ixbe. In 1996, he founded the first Festival de Jonglage Contemporain et Improvisè, held at the Theatre 71 in Malakoff (Paris), where different juggling teams and solo players performed with their own shows. Jerome Thomas' most emotional work, Quartet, premiered in 1999: showcasing "contact-juggling and improvising" with silicone balls. It was a dialogue between the human partners (Thomas, Philippe Menard, Martin Schwietzke, and Emmanuel Anglaret) and the balls. The 90-minute show ended with a unique finale, in which 1,200 balls fall from the heavens to form a white carpet on stage.

At the same time that he created the shows, he became a professor of juggling (1989/90) at the Ecole Superiore des Arts du Cirque at Châlon-sur-Marne, where he taught courses and laboratories. Jerome, the first western juggler to have received this priv-

JÖRG MÜLLER

ilege, has even been invited to conduct juggling courses at the prestigious Moscow Circus School. Among his many pupils we shall just name Philippe Menard and Simon Anxolabèhère, who performed shows directed by him. However, there are many artists who have had Jerome just as a street companion, a "big brother," who then dedicated themselves to researching their own style, as in the case of Jean Daniel Fricker, who unites juggling techniques to those of yoga and butho dance in a completely new combination.

INTERDISCIPLINARY JUGGLERS

The performance artists have created new forms of juggling. At the forefront of this movement was Airjazz, formed in 1982. Working out of Boulder, Colorado, Airjazz's members (Peter Davison, Kezia Tenenbaum, and Jon Held) developed their own style, combining elements of dance with juggling and the manipulation of all kinds of objects to create the fascinating images that made up the troupe's 90-minute show. Airjazz set a high standard for team juggling, working extensively with a wide variety of music. The creative mixture of prop manipulation with body movement this three-person troupe employed made them favorites among their fellow jugglers. They performed with both conventional and nonconventional props as they found inspiration from sources outside the juggling world.

Entirely new areas of juggling are being explored by Peter Davison, who has been performing for 20 years and who rose to fame as a member of Airjazz. He performs a dance piece with a ball, stick, and hoop. Since 1993, Jon Held has been choreographing several large (10-to-20-person) juggling productions for the annual IJA public shows. These performances embody the new trends of the 1990's, and exploration and innovation are two dominant themes driving many of the young European jugglers today. A wonderful, magical innovation is Jörg Müller's metal-tube creation. This German artist performs with five tubes, which hang vertically from strings. As the tubes are swung (juggled) in various arcing patterns, he taps them occasionally, producing sounds. Müller, who graduated in 1994 from Centre National des Arts du Cirque in Châlon-sur-Marne, has worked for three years with Mads Rosenbeck from Denmark.

Another example of today's juggler is Jay Gilligan, from the United States. He is not only a highly technical juggler with balls and clubs, but he is also a very creative juggler in the avant-garde style. Akihiro Matsuura, from Japan, works with up to six balls by juggling and rolling them inside a large crystal-clear globe, his hands and balls weaving in complex patterns and rhythms. Sean Gandini is the founder of the Gandini Juggling Project. Based in London he teamed up with top-class jugglers and well-known choreographers with the aim of combining dance and movement with object manipulations. For the 13th British Juggling Convention Public Show in York, April 2000, Sean Gandini choreographed a 12-person ball-and-club passing piece.

The early 1980's saw the development in America of silicone balls, which have a particularly high bounce. Since then, there has been a boom in the number of jugglers doing ball bouncing. Outstanding specialists in this art of ball bouncing are Argelio Herrera and his son, Miguel, of Cuba, and Antonio Bucci of Italy. Bucci bounced nine balls in 1991

JAY GILLIGAN

AKIHIRO MATSUURA

THE FLYING KARAMAZOV BROTHERS: HOWARD PATTERSON, PAUL MAGID, ROD KIMBALL, MARK ETTINGER, 2002

for the first time, and set a world record in 2001 for bouncing seven balls for 47 minutes, 30 seconds. The trademark of Russian artist Soslan Souanov is also bouncing up to nine balls. Tim Nolan, from the United States, was a record-holder in 1988 for his bouncing with 10 balls. Ben Jennings, from England, set the record for bouncing balls between two people by bouncing 15 balls in 1997 with Morten Hansen, from the United States, and in 1998 with Jay Gilligan, again, from the United States.

No other act has used music with the complexity and diversity demonstrated by the Flying Karamazov Brothers. This American group introduced music into their shows by wearing gloves with metal bars that made the sounds of club catches audible to the audience. The group varied the musical rhythms with different combinations of single and double spins, and added bells to the clubs. They also performed elaborate pieces involving bouncing balls off of multiple tuned drums while juggling and passing the balls.

---

1 De Marinis, Marco, *Il nuovo teatro 1947-1970*, Milano, Bompiani, Sonzogno, 1987, p. 310. (According to De Marinis, the busiest years happened between 1964 and 1968.)

IX

REVIVAL OF NEW VARIETY THEATRES

THE CLASSICAL APPROACH

The traditional market, regarding the years after the war, seems to have made a come-back. It is focused towards a less-informed audience, and the artists become a sort of disposable circus and variety, where the consumers don't go to see that juggler or that artist but a juggler and an artist—anybody, a little like the discount supermarket chains where consumers buy cleansers or cheese and bread without worrying about the quality. In the ambiance of these circuits in the last decades there have been born or have been re-affirmed valuable new circuses that didn't exist between the two World Wars that are now able to host high-level jugglers.

The circuits of the large venues deserve a separate discourse: the Lido and the Moulin Rouge in Paris; the colossal casinos in Las Vegas; the South African Sun City; or a few other large capital cities of the Middle East. Places where show business accompanies massive gambling tourism. It is very difficult to imagine that such expensive shows could survive far away from these highly productive circuits. Furthermore, the audience at such performances consider these shows a mere appendix to their travel motives. The jugglers who perform in these venues are nearly always soloists, coming from traditional families and gifted with good technique. Above all, they possess a certain elegance often combined with a good sense of humor and excellent stage presence.

LAJOS NEREUS

OLIVER GROSZER

On the other hand, the variety theatre network is making a comeback. Venues that seemed destined for extinction are now conversely becoming more successful, principally in Germany, where one can see a constant opening of new venues and re-opening of old and famous ones. A key figure appeared in 1988, the Tiger Palast in Frankfurt, followed in 1992 by the Berlin Wintergarten Variety. Today, there are approximately 17 new variety theatres in Germany, as well as some restaurant mirror-tent shows where spectators can enjoy a good performance.

The opening of these new venues has created an important market for jugglers and with it, an incentive that even if not yet comparable to that of centuries past, brings an improvement and an enrichment to the jugglers' repertoires that are chosen for these networks. The spectator is more cautious and demanding and in general the variety theatres welcome both traditional jugglers and jugglers from other backgrounds.

JUGGLERS OF THE NEW MILLENNIUM

Newcomers of the 1990's who bring youthful individualism to their work with clubs, rings and balls are Stephane Gruss, Lajos Nereus and Valentino Bihorac. Stephane Gruss, also a horseback juggler, descends from a fifth-generation French circus family. Highly technical juggler Lajos Nereus from Hungary and Valentino Bihorac from Bosnia perform with up to 10 rings. American Jason Garfield performs classical, technical juggling, along with comedy. An example of the new breed of juggler is Oliver Groszer, who was born in Berlin. He

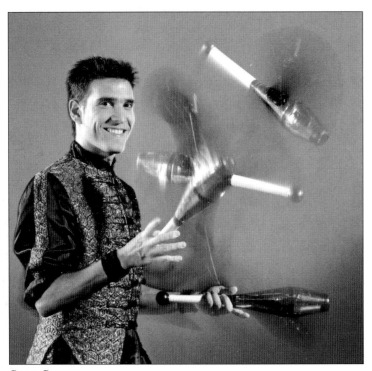

PAUL PONCE

takes clubs and balls out of his suitcase and sends them spinning through the air and around his body. His performances are amusing sketches in which his props take on a life of their own.

Picaso Junior from Spain starts his act by bouncing three and then four ping-pong balls on a paddle held in one hand. The trademark routine from Tuan Le is hat juggling. He was born in Vietnam, but has lived since childhood in Berlin. Highlights of his act include five-hat pancake

TUAN LE AND THE THREE CASTORS

throws and a six-hat juggle. In 1996, with the 3 Castors (Charly, Eddy, Toly), Tuan Le recreated the Elgins' classic hat routine. Paul Ponce, from Argentina, followed in his father's (Victor Ponce) footsteps and presents a similar act. He performs an amazingly fast and complex three-club routine, and works his way up to five, starting the routine by showering the clubs and doing back-throws. His closing hat routine includes six hats thrown out like Frisbees in a large circle.

Mario Berousek descends from a famous seventh-generation Czechoslovakian circus family. He has performed in the circus for 11 years, first appearing with his parents, Fredy and Sonja Berousek, and his brother, Robert, in a club-passing act known as the 4 Fredis. Mario Berousek has been working as a solo performer since 1996 and is today the fastest juggler with up to seven clubs. From the circus school in Cesenatico, Italy, comes Gabriel Agosti, who juggles small balls with his feet, and Willy Colombaioni, who works with balls, rings and up to seven clubs. Claudias Specht from Basel, Switzerland gets his clubs delivered out of a mechanical prop box and is the only person to work with six to ten cocktail shaker cups.

MARIO BEROUSEK

LUKA LUKA

VLADIMIR TSARKOV

Luke Wilson, from England, is a specialist with clubs and he performs solo and also in a duo with his partner Ilka Licht, from Germany, as the team LukaLuka. Both graduated in 1997 from the Circus Space circus school in London. Luke Wilson has also worked with The Gandini Juggling Project. Together, they created lots of new club balances while passing clubs. Feeding the Fish, a trio from England, demonstrate the potential of programmable clubs with built-in lights that change color in time with the formations and tricks, or disappear completely when stuffed into rucksacks for choreographic effect.

A surreal world of clowning and juggling is created by the Companie Les Objets Volants (Denis Paumier, Toon Schuermans and David Fisher). The trio, who graduated from the Centre National des Arts du Cirque in Châlons-sur-Marne (France), specialize in club passing. The identical twins Jake and Marty LaSalle, from the United States, have been juggling for only three years and have been involved in gymnastics for seven. Their act combines acrobatics with club passing and it has been coached by Benji Hill. In 1999, the Teslenkos, from Russia, won the top prize at the Junior Circus Festival's Premiere Rampe, held in Monte Carlo. The rather-likable Teslenko brothers (Dimitri, Anatoli, and Anatolievich) perform a team-juggling act using rings, clubs, and large hoops.

Three Russian juggling acts come from the studio of Valentin Gneouchev in Moscow. Youri Borzykine, from the Ukraine, shows a unique trick while standing on a large globe. He balances a pole on his forehead; atop the pole sits a platform—and on the platform bounces a ball. As all of this is going on, Youri juggles five large balls. Valentin Gneouchev likes to create characters for his performers, so Vladimir Tsarkov, from Russia, became The Red Harlequin, named after Picasso's famous painting. His skill as a contortionist allows him to catch his hoops in any posture imaginable, using his feet, hands, or head.

Ruslan Fomenko, from the Ukraine, has a hypnotically graceful style in a folk costume. His only props are pairs of volleyball-sized balls joined together by a three-foot rope called sviaska. He juggles up to five of these objects. Viktor Kee from the Ukraine, the maestro in acrobatics and silicon balls, is pioneering a new style in his routine with up to seven balls, in which he incorporates his juggling with contortion, acrobatics and movement. He graduated from the Kiev Circus School in 1989, and his teacher was none other than Alex Grusin, known as Petrovich. In practice sessions, Viktor juggles up to nine balls. Four years ago he joined Cirque du Soleil (Dralion Show) where his act was refined until it became the work of art it is today.

Vladik Miagkostoupov, born in the Ukraine but now living in the United States, combines ball and club juggling with acrobatic dance. His father, Anatoli Miagkostoupov, along with partner Victor Pilipovich created in the mid-'80s a new five-club routine in which the clubs were exchanged sideways, backwards, or under the legs from one partner to the other without interrupting the pattern. Vladik juggles up to eight balls and performs also on a free-standing ladder.

Two outstanding Russian female jugglers are Gena Shvartsman and Kristina Kokorina, who juggle up to eight balls. Francoise Rochais, from France, is the only woman who regularly performs with up to seven baton-style clubs. The work with three objects—balls, top hats and cigar boxes—plays an important part in the performance of Kristian Kristof, from Hungary, and Shirley Dean, from Austria, both of whom were born into circus families.

Not all modern cigar-box jugglers are content to explore only myriad possibilities with three cigar boxes. Curiosity and creativity goad them into experimenting with higher numbers, as has been the case in all styles of juggling throughout the years. The American jugglers Charlie Brown and Jeff Daymont became the first to juggle four cigar boxes.

RUSLAN FOMENKO

VLADIK MIAGKOSTOUPOV

DONALD GRANT

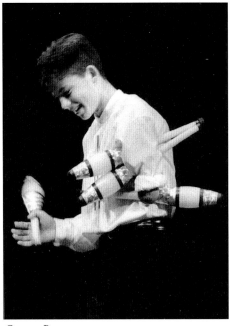

CASEY BOEHMER

In 1995, Orton, from the Czech Republic, and Konstantin Volkov, from Russia, invented many new five-box tricks.

The development of the rubber diabolo revolutionized the art in the mid-1980's, bringing an almost forgotten prop back to center stage. Jochen Schell, from Germany, was one of the early modern diabolo players in Europe. He performs this prop with a new approach that breaks away from the traditional Chinese style of diabolo play. Also from Germany is Martin Mall, who works with illuminated diabolos. Alessandro Traisci, half part of the team Double Face, based in Italy, is the only artist who performs with four diabolos; and Donald Grant, from Scotland, is the author of six instructional booklets on diabolo. Another very popular prop with today's jugglers is the devil stick, masterly performed by Volker Maria Maier, from Germany.

One might think that only having one arm would seriously limit what could be performed in the world of juggling, but American Casey Boehmer proves that even basic natural equipment is not a serious limitation in this art. Casey performs mostly as a member of the 12-person Boehmer Family Jugglers act. Casey began to juggle in earnest at the age of 12, in 1991. In his act, he starts with three clubs, then gets two more and flashes five clubs in one hand. He does a three-ball routine which ends in a double pirouette, as well as several different throws with five beanbags. Casey's final trick is a flash with six rings, in which he takes three rings from his left arm appendage.

We have investigated throughout this book all the inventiveness, hard work and aspirations achieved in the art of juggling. Jugglers never fail to continually surprise audiences with numerous routine variations—seen the world over, from circuses to variety stages, and from street corners to cruise ships. Illustrious jugglers have all helped to enrich the art of juggling and if you tried to list all jugglers who nowadays distinguish themselves by constantly improving their achievements, you would have an almost endless list.

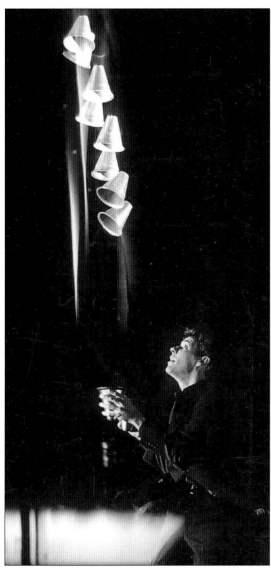

Claudius Specht

Double Face

Stéphane Gruss

Youri Borzykine

Volker Maria Maier

BACK, LEFT TO RIGHT: OLIVER GROSZER, JOCHEN SCHELL, MICHIEL HESSELING, ANDREAS WESSELS, BIHORAC VALENTINO, TUAN LE, DETA, TOM NODDY, LAJOS NEREUS; FRONT, TILL PÖHLMANN, HACKI GINDA, DINO LAMPA; SITTING, AUTHOR KARL-HEINZ ZIETHEN AND KRIS KREMO AT THE PRESENTATION OF THE BOOK "WORLD GREATEST JUGGLERS IN THE CHAMÄLEON VARIETÉ," BERLIN, SEPTEMBER 1996

EPILOGUE

Ever since the very first jugglers amused, astonished and enraptured their audiences with lavish performances and intricate routines, the art of juggling has been a continuous chain of turns and surprises. Over time, jugglers have introduced one "miracle" after another, a constant flow of amazing and novel spectacles. Often, the art of juggling gets delicately passed from generation to generation, with routines constantly evolving and being improved upon with fresh and exciting adaptations. One can only imagine what incredible performances await future audiences.

Jugglers, always the resilient virtuosos, will no doubt continue to strive for the highest originality in their performances, as did those who came before them—a most noteworthy trait that has made jugglers so naturally fascinating to audiences throughout time.

www.renegadejuggling.com

A NOTE FROM THE PUBLISHERS...
RENEGADE JUGGLING

By publishing *Virtuosos of Juggling* we felt that an important historiography of significant jugglers throughout the ages has come to light. There are amazingly few books on juggling such as this one, that is, books containing considerable information regarding jugglers as professionals and juggling as an artform. We wanted our book to be, foremost, a book suitable for anyone enchanted by jugglers and juggling.

Through these pages, you learn the history of our artform, appreciate the performance demands placed upon jugglers due to ever-changing audience appetites, view delightful photographs and graphics (some of which are practically nonexistent), discover jugglers you're unfamiliar with, yet who deserve your admiration, and travel through their lives and witness their demanding routines, practice schedules, specialties, and their impact on the course of juggling from antiquity until today. There are plenty of How-To books relating to juggling, but our book is most unique because it is about juggling's *who* and *why*.

We believe that juggling is an extraordinary artform, like painting or music. *Virtuosos of Juggling* is ideal reading for those who have chosen juggling as a method for expressing themselves. Juggling is not particularly a sport, but overall, it is an artform and a framework for personal expression. Through books such as ours, the art of juggling is kept alive—and its greatest practitioners can never be forgotten.

Juggling is a meaningful "life tool" because it trains a person fully—physically and mentally. Juggling is great for all ages, including children. Everyone can learn to juggle. You don't have to become a master and perfect the art to experience juggling's benefits: creative inspiration, artistic cognizance, physical fitness, strength, patience, dexterity, focus, and the development of both sides of your brain.

We believe that juggling does wonderful things for your soul. Juggling keeps your personal creativity vibrant. When you juggle, you realize your goals by practice and concentration. You encounter personal success. You sense exhilaration when you learn how to perform a particular juggling routine, and each time you perform your routine in front of others, you feel that excitement all over again. Juggling is a highly emotional activity... your success is emotionally attached to you.

We hope you enjoy reading *Virtuosos of Juggling* as much as we enjoyed creating and publishing it.

— Tom Kidwell and Iman Lizarazu

Renegade Juggling offers a full line of professional juggling equipment for all skill levels. Many jugglers who perform professionally throughout the world, and jugglers who have set world records, such as Anthony Gatto, use Renegade Juggling products. You can visit Renegade Juggling and view our custom-made products at www.renegadejuggling.com.

TRANSLATOR'S AFTERWORD

It's a startling change to have a book originally written in Italian and see it translated into English—because it's usually the other way around. Most often, books in English are translated into Italian. When a book of this distinction is written, it is necessary to translate it into English so that it may be shared with the English-speaking world.

When it comes to literature on juggling, Italians normally get by with English and French editions. As you will soon find out, this is not an ordinary book—but a voyage into the evolution of our art. I was very pleased to translate this book, even if it took training-time away from me. After reading and translating this book, I will most certainly train in a different way from now on. (I must thank my mother, Christine, who lives in England, for going over the manuscript and sorting out my slightly tricky English.)

Admittedly, if I hadn't had to translate this volume I would have probably just flicked though the beautiful illustrations, skimmed a little bit of the text and then, somewhat proudly, put it on my bookshelf. Instead, having practically studied and memorized the book, it would be a real pity just to look at the photos. This is a history book, and the history of juggling unfolds as you read the text. The artists are sterling examples of consummate performers during the colorful history of juggling. For me, it is amazing to see the way history unravels itself. It is always humbling to realize that our era isn't really a great deal different from many years ago... the main problems are nearly always the same.

We often feel, however, that we are somehow different—what will happen 100 years from now—and what will be left of our juggling art? From a professional viewpoint, it's essential to learn how the artists adapted in their own times, to win the favor of the audiences or not. Is technical skill really enough for today's lay public, or do we need to package juggling in some other way?

Do we truly understand what sort of power and energy that jugglers throughout history were able to project? What is the rapport between breathing and juggling? What happens when everything works together easily and spontaneously? What happens if we want to be the best at all costs? How do we deal with the audience's expectations? There are many other unanswered questions, too—such as, why do jugglers get bad press so often? When we train, what are our motivations? Do we even know how to train? We sometimes find ourselves juggling and learning on our own, whereas juggling possibly could be taken much further with proper study and understanding.

Let's not think that the history of juggling has already ended. If we use our heads, juggling has just begun...
—Anthony Trahair

Anthony Trahair has lived in Rome since 1997, and he has completely dedicated himself to juggling and performing arts.

NAME & PHOTOGRAPH INDEX

HISTORICAL MEETING WHEN BOB BRAMSON PERFORMED AT THE TIGER PALAST ON NOV. 2, 1991 IN FRANKFURT. TOP ROW: KARL-HEINZ ZIETHEN, TOLY CASTOR, SERGEI IGNATOV, OLIVER GROSZER; BOTTOM ROW: BOB BRAMSON, FRANCIS BRUNN & ERNEST MONTEGO.

*NATHALIE ENTERLINE, DANIELLE GATTO, TOP;
ANTHONY GATTO, KARL-HEINZ ZIETHEN, FRANCIS BRUNN,
BOTTOM; AT TIGER PALAST, 2000.*